Praise for *Total Family Makeover*

"We are happy to award deserving books like *Total Family Makeover*. Our panel of judges really felt this book merited a place on our list of the best in family-friendly products that parents can feel confident in using."

—**Dawn Matheson**, Executive Director, Mom's Choice Awards

"Do you want your children to love Jesus and follow Him forever? While there are no magic formulas, in the Bible God gives you specific things you can do toward the mission of impressing the hearts of your kids with a love for God. This book is full of those biblical principles and action steps! You will come away with simple but powerful practices that will bless your family for generations to come."

—**Dr. Rob Rienow**, founder Visionary Family Ministries, author of *Visionary Parenting*

"So many of us moms are overwhelmed by our daily responsibilities and intimidated by the idea of teaching our children about Jesus and the Bible. Melissa encourages us to be confident and intentional in our training and to be thankful for all our mommy experiences. Through her fun family stories, she shares practical and creative ways to give our children the knowledge of God's love, each day."

—**Gina San Martin**, MOPS Leadership Team

"We parents are so busy devouring books on how to get our kids on elite sports teams or into the best schools for their future that we might be missing establishing the core values they will need to literally survive. This practical handbook for busy parents offers easy steps we can do today to ensure a better tomorrow for our children. Melissa writes with a practical no-nonsense approach that I find relatable and refreshing. It's a 'don't miss' book for any household!"

—**Kerri Pomarolli**, comedian, actress, and author of *Moms' Night Out and Other Things I Miss*

Melissa Spoelstra

Total Family
MAKEOVER

Practical Steps to Making Disciples
at Home

Abingdon Press

Nashville

TOTAL FAMILY MAKEOVER
8 PRACTICAL STEPS TO MAKING DISCIPLES AT HOME

Copyright © 2016 by Abingdon Press

Library of Congress Cataloging-in-Publication Data has been requested.
ISBN 978-1-5018-2065-6

16 17 18 19 20 21 22 23 24 25—10 9 8 7 6 5 4 3 2 1
MANUFACTURED IN THE UNITED STATES OF AMERICA

To my mentor Deb Taylor. You are who I want to be when I grow up. Your authenticity, generosity, and love for people is contagious. Thank you for loving me so well for so many years and showing me what a family following Jesus looks like!

CONTENTS

FOREWORD

I have struggled with nighttime anxiety for years. I wake up and I think of all the ways in which I'm failing as a mom and what I need to do to be better. There's so much it seems, and I keep dropping the ball. I feel responsible to teach and train my children, and it's true: I am responsible. God made me my kids' mom. But I have been carrying a weight God didn't intend. I can't be a perfect mom, and I won't get it all right. I remember I had a mentor in college and I asked her, "What do you wish you would have done better as a parent?" And she answered, "I would have done everything right." Isn't that just the thing? We wish we could get it all right? But Melissa reminds us in *Total Family Makeover* that even though God modeled perfect parenting, and He loved perfectly, His children still disobeyed. We can guide and instruct and do our best with who we are and what our capacity is, through God's grace and strength, but at the end of the day, we cannot save our children. We cannot carry the weight of their ultimate behavior, whether good or bad. It's the Lord's kindness and grace and the work of the Holy Spirit that will mold their hearts for His glory.

But there is still this instruction in Scripture to teach and train our children. And I want to tell them about the God I love, but sometimes I feel like I'm floundering. How exactly do I disciple my children? For some of us, discipleship in a family was never modeled. Maybe like me, you weren't brought up in a Christian family and so you're figuring it all out as you go along. You're not alone. Or maybe you were in a wonderful Christian family, but you still feel a bit lost. Melissa offers us a practical, grace-filled "track" as she calls it to run on. She shows us through example and Scripture eight ways to disciple our children. And it doesn't feel heavy or legalistic, but doable and true and freedom-based. I love how Melissa encourages us to shift our focus from our children's behavior to the joy-filled adventure of teaching them. Yes, that's what I want! I want to experience joy and freedom in teaching and leading them to God's heart so that they may know Him intimately.

> *And Solomon, my son, learn to know the God of your ancestors intimately. Worship and serve him with your whole heart and a willing mind. For the LORD sees every heart and knows every plan and thought. If you seek him, you will find him.*
>
> (1 Chronicles 28:9a)

Total Family Makeover is much-needed truth for moms. Melissa's words are like hands that gently lift the heavy burden so many of us wear.

As she says, God doesn't grade himself according to his children's successes and failures, and neither should we.

Enjoy this book, friends, it is a gift. We don't need to make discipling complicated or painstaking or figure it all out perfectly. We begin by taking one step. And then a second. And when we're ready, a third. Let this beautiful book be one of your guides.

Sarah Mae
Coauthor of *Desperate: Hope for the Mom Who Needs to Breathe*

INTRODUCTION

Your Kids Are Not Your Report Card

O ne day during church a children's ministry leader motioned for me to leave the service with her. In the hallway, she asked if I knew the parents of a certain child and requested my help in locating them. Their daughter had been scratched in the face by another three-year-old in class, and she needed to inform the parents. She didn't know the details or which child was the scratcher. When we arrived at the classroom, I discovered that my daughter had been the culprit! After profusely apologizing to the parents, I packed up all four of my kids and scooted home as quickly as possible. I felt that if I were to get a "mom grade" that day, it would be an F.

Another time I sat in a school assembly during which they awarded the citizen of the year award to only one third-grader in the entire school. When my son was chosen, I beamed. Arriving home after being congratulated many times over, I felt like an A parent—at least until one of the twins threw a tantrum.

It's easy to fall into the trap of seeing our kids as our report cards. God calls us to answer their questions, train them, and lovingly discipline them without exasperating them. So when they obey, that must mean we are succeeding; and when they disobey, we've missed the mark. Right?

Wrong. I've come to understand and embrace something profound. God modeled perfect parenting. He walked in the garden in close relationship with Adam and Eve. He clearly trained them, giving instructions about which tree was off-limits. Even though he loved his children perfectly, they still disobeyed. God continues to discipline, instruct, and walk with his children. But he doesn't grade himself according to his children's successes and failures. And neither should we.

When we use the behavior of our children as our parenting measuring rod, we find ourselves

- passing judgment on others when their children struggle, rather than encouraging and praying for them;
- yo-yoing between pride and shame according to our children's behavior;
- envying our friends when we read social media posts about the academic, athletic, and other achievements of their kids.

The result is disappointment and discouragement. So what can we do? How can we shift our focus from our children's behavior to the joy-filled adventure of teaching them what it means to follow Jesus? How can we give ourselves a total family makeover as we seek to train our children in the faith and make disciples at home?

I find that I compare, measure, and worry less when I hold onto this promise from Proverbs 22:6 (NKJV): "Train up a child in the way he should go, / And when he is old he will not depart from it." God calls us to do all we can to train our children spiritually, but the goal is not their perfect behavior now; it is their desire to follow him long after they have left home. Rather than worrying about how we're doing in the moment, we need to strive to lead our kids to know and love God over the long haul. How? I believe the answer is to teach them the spiritual practices or disciplines that will help them down the path of loving God.

Now, that can be an overwhelming thought, because we're not sure where to begin and wonder if we'll forget something important. We might hope that grandparents or the church would do this important job for us, but the truth is that the primary responsibility for the spiritual nurturing of our children resides with us and begins at home. Just as we are careful to take care of our children physically, in the same way we can be intentional in modeling and teaching good spiritual practices. We just need a way to begin—a "track to run on," if you will.

I've found great success in other areas of life by having a track to run on. In finances, for example, my husband and I found a place to begin and a system for slowly working through the steps toward financial health. Those steps have required patience, flexibility, and perseverance through the years, but they have produced real changes in our spending, saving, and giving. The same is true when it comes to nurturing our children spiritually. With patience, flexibility, and perseverance, we can follow some basic steps that over time will transform our families—beginning with us!

This book gives you a track to run on by suggesting eight practical steps to making disciples at home. These steps revolve around basic spiritual practices or habits that we want our children to embrace in their walk with God—both now and after they leave home. Each chapter in this book focuses on one of these eight practices:

1. **Spending time in prayer.** Jesus modeled the practice of prayer and taught his disciples how to pray. After looking at these biblical examples, you'll find practical ideas to enhance your own conversations with God as well as a guide to use in teaching your child to pray— tools that will equip your family to follow Jesus into the practice of prayer.

2. **Reading God's Word.** Just as our children require physical food, we also need to help them learn to feed themselves spiritually. As you let biblical truth sink deeply into your own life, you can share what you are learning with your child through a simple daily application. You'll also find practical ways to implement daily Bible reading into your

busy schedule as well as help your child discover the power of the living Word of God in his or her own life.

3. **Growing through mentoring.** Jesus demonstrated the importance of mentoring through his relationship with his disciples. He taught and encouraged them as they did life together, pouring into them until they were ready to be on their own. You are your child's first mentor. After discussing how to find a Christian parenting mentor for yourself, we'll apply those principles to coaching your child. Suggestions for special dates with your child as well as mentoring questions will enhance your relationship with your child. Children who are mentored at home learn the value of this important spiritual discipline and are more likely to seek out spiritual mentoring relationships when they are grown.

4. **Finding community in the church.** God loves community. We are designed to live in relationship with others, not in isolation. Today we see a shift in the cultural view of the posture and purposes of the church. In order to prevent our kids from looking at the church as a commodity to be consumed, we need to be intentional in teaching them to find a place where they can connect with other believers and participate through worship, fellowship, and service. You'll find ideas for helping your child develop nourishing friendships as well as ways to foster intergenerational relationships within the church.

5. **Serving others.** Jesus showed us that joy comes from serving. We'll examine his example and see how our lives can reflect his attitude of service. Just as Jesus taught his disciples to serve through hands-on practice, we'll consider ways that we can include our children in serving opportunities. A serving debrief worksheet will help you follow through in seeing your child realize the pleasure to be found in helping others.

6. **Taking time to rest.** With our hectic lives, we often unconsciously teach our kids that they should fill every waking hour with activity. Yet Jesus valued rest. We'll take a look at the Sabbath concept from the Old Testament and how that translates into New Testament living.

You'll find help for identifying the unique ways each person in your family experiences leisure best by trying some simple ideas, such as taking a walk together, heading out into nature, or putting away electronics so that you can engage in conversation.

7. **Giving back to God.** In a world consumed with having more, our children need guidance when it comes to money. Jesus had plenty to say about finances. He warned about the dangers of loving money and celebrated the blessings of generosity. You'll find ideas for age-appropriate chores and encouragement to incorporate regular compensation so that your child can learn the value of saving as well as the rewards of generosity.

8. **Sharing your faith.** One of the marks of a disciple is the ability to "reproduce." Jesus commissioned his disciples to tell others about him. Our children need instruction for sharing what they believe with respect and kindness. In a world that labels Christians as judgmental and pushy with our beliefs, we want our kids to understand that our desire for others to know Jesus springs from our love for them. You'll find help for sharing your own faith as well as age-appropriate ideas for teaching children how to make this important practice a natural part of their lives and relationships.

Certainly this isn't an exhaustive list of spiritual disciplines, but these eight basic habits will provide a strong foundation for growing in faith. They are meant to be a lifelong pursuit, not a list to check off and then expect instant results. Whether our children embrace Christ or any of these disciplines isn't up to us. So instead of worrying about how they respond, we can shift our focus to our own spiritual habits and seek to be intentional and consistent in both modeling an authentic relationship with God and training our children in his ways. With prayer and persistence, we can be confident that God will honor our efforts and begin to transform our lives, our families, and our homes.

In the following pages you'll find a very practical approach. Each chapter has two major sections, Modeling and Training, and includes Scriptures to help us see how Jesus modeled and trained his own disciples in the practice.

You'll find help and suggestions for modeling the habit yourself, as well as pro-active ways you can focus more on the task of training your child in the spiritual practice. Practical ideas and activities are highlighted throughout with the heading "A Practical Approach."

We don't have to know all the answers, but we can be open and ready. Our children need us to dialogue with them, listen, and help them learn the spiritual disciplines that will draw them closer to God. Jesus said, "Go and make disciples of all the nations, baptizing them in the name of the Father and the Son and the Holy Spirit" (Matthew 28:19). Notice the word *make*. Disciples are made, not born. Our kids will not automatically default to a life of prayer, serving, and generosity. God calls us as parents to be key disciple-makers in our children's lives.

Whether you have a babe in arms, a toddler, a tween, or a teen, I encourage you to go beyond reading this book. Resolve to implement some of the ideas and activities. Plan some family service projects, use the worksheets provided, or take the challenge to spend time with God every day for thirty days. Ask yourself the tough questions about what you are modeling. Are you spending the amount of time with God each day that you hope your children will spend with him when they are grown? Get alongside some other parents and encourage one another to persevere in modeling and training for a real relationship with God. (You'll find group discussion questions and study helps at the end of each chapter.)

Together we can make God our parenting audience of one so that we care more about what he thinks about our kids than what the watching world thinks. So the next time you're concerned about a disrespectful tone or a bad test score, don't give yourself an F in parenting for the day. Instead, pray for perspective and persistence to keep loving and parenting with complete dependence on the Holy Spirit's guidance. And remember, God calls us to be faithful to him, not to produce perfect children. Though we are instructed to train and lead them to Jesus, our kids are not our report card. That frees us to parent them with love and patience, trusting God to do the rest!

CHAPTER 1

SPENDING TIME IN PRAYER

My twelve-year-old daughter sobbed as she asked why all of her hair was falling out. I held her close and wept with her. She told me she talked to God about it all the time, but he didn't seem to be answering. It can be rough to help our children learn to hear God's voice—especially during seasons when he seems silent.

The good news is that we don't have to make excuses for God or be embarrassed about his apparent lack of communication. He is real, and he does speak to us. At times we may not understand, but we can help our children learn to seek God in prayer.

When my daughter's hair was falling out due to an autoimmune disorder called alopecia, I searched his Word to hear what truth we could cling to in the situation. He doesn't promise to always heal, but he does say that he is a rewarder of those who sincerely seek him (Hebrews 11:6). God's Word also says, "The eyes of the LORD search the whole earth in order to strengthen those whose hearts are fully committed to him" (2 Chronicles 16:9a). These are truths we can rely on—especially when God may seem quiet in our difficult circumstances.

Kids are great about being honest when they don't feel as though they hear God. Recently I taught a Sunday school class the story of Elijah. In

1 Kings 19, God says he will show himself to Elijah. First there is a mighty wind, then an earthquake, and afterward a fire. Yet God was not in any of those things. He was in the still small voice. I encouraged the boys and girls in my class not to always look for God in big, showy ways but to spend a few moments every day getting quiet before him. We took a minute to just sit quietly and practice listening. I loved it when a sweet six-year-old boy jumped up immediately afterward and proclaimed, "Well, I didn't hear God say a thing!"

There is no magic formula for hearing God. There's no checklist that will guarantee a message from the Lord. Still, we can cultivate a relationship with God that creates room for dialogue. When we know someone well, our conversations move to greater depth and intimacy as we share our joys and fears with them. But how do we get to know a God we can't see? Just as we deepen our relationships with others through spending time together and dialoguing about things that are important to us, so we can get to know God better by spending focused time with him.

MODELING

Let's look at the example Jesus set for us by spending time in prayer.

1. Jesus intentionally pulled away from other responsibilities to spend time alone with the Father.

Jesus left some very worthy pursuits to make time with his Father a priority. His disciples needed direction. The sick needed healing. The hungry wanted food. The crowds were anxious for teaching. Yet Jesus purposely abandoned these tasks to demonstrate our need for time alone with God.

Sometimes Jesus prayed in the early morning hours: "Before daybreak the next morning, Jesus got up and went out to an isolated place to pray" (Mark 1:35). Other times he stayed up late into the night to pray: "After sending them home, he went up into the hills by himself to pray. Night fell while he was there alone" (Matthew 14:23). We also learn from Luke's Gospel that

Jesus prayed frequently: "Jesus *often* withdrew to the wilderness for prayer" (Luke 5:16, my emphasis). Jesus set the example for us, showing us our need to connect with God in prayer. I believe that in addition to communing with the Father, Jesus wanted us to know that time spent talking and listening with God is vital to a disciple of Christ.

As parents, our greatest enemy of time in prayer is often the endless list of tasks and responsibilities. The laundry buzzes; the phone rings; the baby cries; the work e-mails pile up; and someone always seems to need another piece of us. The tyranny of other things can be our biggest barrier to time alone with God. Yet Jesus, the Son of God, who went place to place teaching, healing, and feeding people, found it important to take time away from those pursuits and make prayer a priority.

As you think through your days, what is God calling you to pull away from for just a few minutes every day so you can spend time with him? God would rather have a few minutes with you than none at all.

I've often made prayer too complicated. I think that if I don't have a good block of time or complete privacy, then I can't pray. Susanna Wesley is said to have sat in her rocking chair with a shawl over her head to spend time with the Lord. When my kids were little, I would sometimes steal away to my room in desperation to get on my knees and pour out my heart to God. After just a few minutes, they would break into the room and climb onto my back, using me for a jungle gym. That was okay. Even just a few minutes of connection with God gave me the strength I needed for the moment. I decided that I would rather have interrupted prayer times than no prayer times at all—and that it was a good thing for them to see me praying.

Making time for prayer may mean getting our sleepy selves up a little earlier in the morning or burning the midnight oil. If we're honest, we make time for what we value. When there is a television show I really want to see, I find the time to watch it. If my budget finally allows for new carpet, I somehow find the time to research the different choices and colors available. If we really want to know God and hear his voice, we will make the sacrifices necessary to connect with him. Jesus modeled it for us so that we could learn to talk with God. In the same way, we can show our kids that prayer is a priority in our lives by doing it.

When was the last time your kids discovered you praying? Whether you were on your knees, on your face, or in the car with your eyes closed while you were waiting for them, your example shows your children that you talk to Jesus regularly. We can model the importance of spending time with God by intentionally laying aside other tasks and pursuits—even good things—to make prayer a priority.

2. Jesus communicated to his disciples that he was praying for them.

Another way Jesus set an example for us was by talking about his prayer life. Now, Jesus was no prayer bragger. Unlike the Pharisees who recited their spiritual pedigrees, Jesus didn't feel the need to make himself seem spiritual by mentioning his long hours in prayer. In fact, it is only because others observed him praying and made mention of it in the Gospels that we have a record of his prayer life. But Jesus wasn't ashamed to tell people he was praying for them. Jesus encouraged Peter with prayer: "But I have pleaded in prayer for you, Simon, that your faith should not fail. So when you have repented and turned to me again, strengthen your brothers" (Luke 22:32).

How do you think it encouraged Simon Peter to know that Jesus was pleading in prayer for him? Has anyone ever stormed the gates of heaven on your behalf?

When my daughter was five years old, she was very ill and spent six days in an intensive care unit. She breathed with a ventilator and fought for her life. The outpouring of support from our church family with meals, notes, and much prayer on her behalf was incredible. But the most memorable and tangible encouragement for me during that time was from a man I had met only once. He sent a note saying he had felt led by the Spirit to take a day off work to fast and pray for my daughter. I still get tears in my eyes just thinking about it. It meant so much to know that someone else was seeking God so fervently on our behalf. Our daughter was healed and completely restored to health. As the years have passed, I've never forgotten the sacrifice of that man.

As I've watched friends, relatives, and my own children walk difficult roads, at times I've communicated with them that I was taking some time to fast and pray on their behalf. When we feel helpless to do something to ease the burdens of others, we can always pray. Prayer is not "nothing." It is a big something!

Not only did Jesus pray for those around him when he walked the earth; he also prayed for *you*! Jesus had a lengthy dialogue with the Father in front of a crowd after teaching about the coming of the Holy Spirit and future events. He said, "I am praying not only for these disciples but also for all who will ever believe in me through their message. I pray that they will all be one, just as you and I are one—as you are in me, Father, and I am in you. And may they be in us so that the world will believe you sent me" (John 17:20-21).

Jesus prayed for everyone who would believe in him. He prayed for you. How does that encourage you? Do you regularly let your children know that you are praying for them? While they may roll their eyes or brush it off, it means something to them.

We occasionally have a family meeting where Sean and I ask everyone to share one prayer request. Then I record their answers in my journal and try to follow up with them later. I want them to know that their dad and I pray for them. The blessing for me is that when I pray more, I tend to worry less. What we model for our children can be caught easily, and I want my children to catch the habit of prayer rather than the habit of worry.

I remember when our youngest daughter used to say the word *ridiculous* as a three-year-old. We all laughed because it was my husband's word of choice when he saw a mess left in the house. He didn't work with her on saying that word. She just heard him say it and started using it herself. That memory makes me laugh, but it also reminds me that I don't want my kids to see me worrying and pick up the habit.

Sometimes it's so hard not to worry, isn't it? Right now I've got a few things rolling around in the back of my mind, threatening to send me into full-on worry mode. Is my son doing okay in college? How are his grades, his laundry, his friendships? How will I respond to that e-mail with tact? Will my daughter ever see God's love in the midst of her alopecia? I want to trust God with every bit of it, but I must wrestle in prayer to actually turn it over to God, just as each of us must.

I can help my kids learn the power of prayer as I tell them how I am praying for them and then back up my example with faith instead of fear. I can be honest with them about the struggle to trust rather than worry, but I must ask myself which one I will let win—faith or fear? Kids are smart. They know when we are wearing a mask and when we really believe what we say. As we lift up their struggles to God, we model for them a life of dependency and trust instead of worry.

A Practical Approach: Praying for Your Child

What is your child facing right now that you need to pray for more consistently?

What's a practical way you can make a more intentional effort to pray for your child?

How will you let your child know that you are praying for him or her? Here are a few ideas:

- Set an alarm on your phone to pray for your child daily. If you have more than one child, choose a different time of the day or a different day of the week to pray for each one.
- Keep a prayer journal with your child's requests.
- Pick one day of the week that you will communicate that you are praying for your child or children.

> • Choose one word for each child as a prayer theme for the year. I have four children, and I am praying for purity for one, humility for another, obedience for another, and healing for my daughter with alopecia. I present specific requests to the Lord as well, but these key words help me focus on broad needs.

3. Jesus taught us to pray in faith.

Jesus told a story to teach about persistent prayer:

> Then, teaching them more about prayer, he used this story: "Suppose you went to a friend's house at midnight, wanting to borrow three loaves of bread. You say to him, 'A friend of mine has just arrived for a visit, and I have nothing for him to eat.' And suppose he calls out from his bedroom, 'Don't bother me. The door is locked for the night, and my family and I are all in bed. I can't help you.' But I tell you this—though he won't do it for friendship's sake, if you keep knocking long enough, he will get up and give you whatever you need because of your shameless persistence" (Luke 11:5-8).

Shameless persistence! He wants us to ask and keep asking. Jesus went on to say, "And so I tell you, keep on asking, and you will receive what you ask for. Keep on seeking, and you will find. Keep on knocking, and the door will be opened to you. For everyone who asks, receives. Everyone who seeks, finds. And to everyone who knocks, the door will be opened" (Luke 11:10-11).

If we want our kids to be the kind of Christ-followers who pray this way, we need to model shameless persistence. We don't give up when the going gets tough as parents. We pray with shameless persistence:

7

- when our child is sick again
- when our marriage gets tough and tougher
- when the finances don't add up
- when we feel like getting a black-and-white-striped shirt because all we do is referee arguing
- when friendships end
- when we have to move

Whatever it is, we keep asking, seeking, and knocking. Rather than a last resort, prayer is what we do with shameless persistence.

- Is there an area in your life that seems out of control?
- How have you been trying to manage it, manipulate it, or fix it yourself?
- How can you begin to model shameless persistence and include your children in the prayer process?

Jesus's story about persistent prayer communicates to us that nothing is too small a reason to beat on God's door. We are not nagging or irritating him when we pray persistently. When my kids ask continually for something, I have to admit, it drives me nuts. But God isn't like me. He is patient and loving and wants us to know that our shameless persistence isn't an irritation. In fact, he welcomes us to confidently come to him: "So let us come boldly to the throne of our gracious God. There we will receive his mercy, and we will find grace to help us when we need it most" (Hebrews 4:16).

It's so incredible to know that we find mercy at God's throne—not judgment or condemnation, but grace when we need it most. Even when we are questioning and doubting, God wants to help us believe. Thomas was one of the disciples who didn't believe Jesus had risen from the dead after the crucifixion. He said he wouldn't believe unless he put his fingers in the nail holes of Christ's hands. Here's what happened: "Eight days later the disciples were together again, and this time Thomas was with them. The doors were locked; but suddenly, as before, Jesus was standing among them. 'Peace be with you,' he said. Then he said to Thomas, 'Put your finger here, and look at my hands. Put your hand into the wound in my side. Don't be faithless any longer. Believe!'" (John 20:26-27).

Notice that Jesus didn't shame Thomas but helped him believe in the midst of his doubts.

- How does Jesus's reaction to Thomas encourage you to press on in prayer?
- In what situations have your doubts kept you from coming to God?
- Take a few moments now to bring any doubts and fears to God, asking Jesus to help you trust him when you can't see.

I hope it encourages you to remember that we can pray and seek God even in the midst of our doubts.

4. Jesus prayed out loud in front of others to build their faith.

We find several instances when Jesus offered public prayers. When his friend Lazarus died, "Jesus looked up to heaven and said, 'Father, thank you for hearing me. You always hear me, but I said it out loud for the sake of all these people standing here, so that they will believe you sent me'" (John 11:41-42). Did you notice why Jesus prayed out loud? He did it to increase the faith of those around him.

When it comes to our own prayer lives, many of us are uncomfortable praying out loud. We feel it is a personal thing. If we are shy and don't like praying in large groups, that is understandable. But when it comes to our own children, we would be wise to get over ourselves and learn to pray alongside our kids. They need to hear us talk to God reverently but also personally and authentically.

Your prayer life can be one of the ways God chooses to build the faith of your child. God can use anything. He spoke through a donkey once, and even the rocks will cry out with praise if we don't worship him. Yet he desires to use *us*. God calls us to be his hands and feet in modeling prayer and training our children in this important habit.

When is the last time you prayed with your child? It's never too early to start. You can start a bedtime prayer routine as you are rocking your infant. It's also never too late. You can begin a daily prayer time with your child at any age. Our family has done different things in different seasons of life. When I drove the kids to school every day, we prayed in the car on the way. We've also had a nighttime prayer habit because it's the most consistent routine of our day. Check out the practical prayer ideas in the Practical Approach section on page 12.

As we pray out loud in front of our children—whether at meals, at bedtime, or in impromptu moments such as when we see a car accident ahead—we can plant seeds of faith that will sprout and bloom in our children's lives. Though we plant the seeds, it is God who makes them grow.

5. Jesus prayed for God's will.

When Jesus faced a time of great suffering, he wanted God's ultimate best instead of immediate ease. In Luke 22 we read, "He walked away, about a stone's throw, and knelt down and prayed, 'Father, if you are willing, please take this cup of suffering away from me. Yet I want your will to be done, not mine'" (vv. 41-42).

This is a tough prayer to pray. I just finished praying with my girls at bedtime. Oh, how I want God to give my daughter hair again. She also has some normal high school struggles. Her twin sister has two bald spots where she, too, has lost hair, which I am asking God to restore. The thought of another girl going through that pain of wigs and fake eyelashes makes me want to scream "NO!" I know alopecia is not the worst thing in the world, but it's our thing. And it's no picnic.

I don't want my kids to suffer. No parent does. But if I really want to pray like Jesus, then after asking with shameless persistence I must add, "Yet I want your will to be done, not mine." I know that his will is best. Jesus's death on the cross brought us freedom from sin and reconciliation with God, but it came at a high price with an amount of suffering we can't even begin to wrap our minds around. Still, he knew the suffering was worth what God would bring through it.

Isaiah 55:9 tells us, "For just as the heavens are higher than the earth, / so my ways are higher than your ways / and my thoughts higher than your thoughts." God may have plans and purposes for things that, from my vantage point, look like useless suffering. As we pray with our children, we boldly ask, but we also surrender our wills to God knowing that sometimes what is gracious from heaven's view seems awfully tough from ours. We are watching through the knothole, but God sees the whole parade.

In prayer we express our deepest longings, but ultimately we must trust God's action or inaction in our lives as his best for us. It sure is easier to write those words than to live them! Sometimes this is where we learn a lesson from our children in choosing simple faith over complicated attempts to understand.

- What prayer request do you have right now that you need to surrender with the words, "Yet I want your will to be done, not mine"?
- How will adding this statement to your prayer times with your children help them to learn that God is not like a cosmic vending machine?
- Can you think of some helpful examples kids can relate to that might help bring this principle to life?

One example that comes to mind for me is the movie *The Karate Kid*. Mr. Miyagi has Daniel doing all kinds of hard work such as washing cars, cleaning floors, and painting fences. Daniel becomes so frustrated, thinking this work has nothing to do with karate. Yet Mr. Miyagi has a plan in mind all along to strengthen his muscles and reflexes, preparing him to fight.

Though God is certainly not the author of evil, sometimes God allows hardships and uses them for his purposes. When it comes to praying God's will over my own, I have to trust that God will bring good even from what is frustrating or difficult at the time.

First Corinthians 15:58 says, "So, my dear brothers and sisters, be strong and immovable. Always work enthusiastically for the Lord, for you know that nothing you do for the Lord is ever useless." If we believe God doesn't waste anything—not our suffering, not the bad things other people do to us, not the good times—we can more easily ask for his will over our own.

Your child may not be familiar with this movie, but he or she can understand a coach who has the team practice hard to prepare for a game. Perhaps your child cares for a pet and realizes that sometimes he has to make the pet do things it doesn't want to do for its own good (such as take baths or stay out of the road). Other kids might relate to the doctor giving them medicine that tastes bad in the moment, but ultimately it will help them get better.

Think of a way you can help explain praying God's will to your child. What story or example can you use from your own life? How can you talk about trusting the heart of someone who has your best interests at heart?

It isn't easy to believe when we can't see or understand the reasons for our pain. But our faith can grow as we seek God in prayer, asking for his will over our own.

- Review the five principles of prayer that Jesus modeled. Which one resonates most in your life right now?
- What is one change you'd like to make related to how you set an example of prayer for your children?

A Practical Approach: Organizing Your Prayer Life

Have you ever felt the sting of wanting to tell someone you prayed for them, but you know you really didn't? How about when you open your notes at Bible study or small group and find where you wrote all the prayer requests from your last meeting, but you haven't prayed about a single one? It's tough to stay on top of our own families' prayer needs, let alone lift up other requests to God! Not only that, but some needs are ongoing (such as our children's spiritual growth or a specific health need) while other needs are short term (such as the sale of a house or the need for a job). How can we keep track of it all?

Since college I have kept some kind of journal or notebook in which I write my thoughts, keep to-do lists, take sermon notes, and organize prayer needs. I use the last few pages in my journal for prayer needs so I don't have to flip through the book to find them.

The first page in this section is for daily requests. I attempt to pray for my husband, my children, and my church every day. (I don't always do it every single day, but this is my desire when I'm in my normal routine.) I write two or three key requests I have for each of them—such as time management for my husband, college concerns for my son, good friends for my daughters, and so forth.

The next page is a weekly list. I assign a day for different things. For example, I might pray for the families in my small group on Wednesday or for my extended family on Friday. This way I don't feel that I need to be praying for everyone, everywhere, every day. (That would be a surefire way never to get started in praying for people!)

The last page is for short-term requests. This page usually has a lot of things that have been crossed off as needs are answered or no longer current. For example, I prayed for my friend's divorce hearing as she asked. When it was over, I drew a line through that request. I also prayed many months for my friend Lee, who was struggling with cancer. When Jesus took him home, I didn't need to pray for his healing anymore, because Lee is fully whole in heaven with his precious Savior. Sometimes things stay on this list for days, weeks, or even a year.

When the rest of my journal is full with written prayers, to-do lists, sermon notes, book ideas, or important phone numbers (which I can never seem to find—not a good system for that!), I decide it's time to get a new journal. I then rewrite my three prayer pages at the back of my new journal. By then it's time to update things and reorganize anyway.

This is just one prayer organization system that has worked for me. Many people use different prayer tools with success.

- Some people keep an electronic prayer journal on their computer or tablet, and others like to use prayer journal apps.
- My husband uses the calendar in his phone to set reminders to pray for different people and situations.
- My mentor, Deb, uses sticky notes. She has them on her bathroom mirror, car dashboard, and different places around her home. She has tried other systems, but she finds she is most consistent with prayer when she has a request on a sticky note.
- Other people write requests on index cards and put them in their Bible. Then when they do their daily Bible reading, they pray for others.
- One of my friends uses her Bible study workbook. She writes requests at the top of the daily homework so she'll see things to pray about during her study time.

There are many different systems for keeping up with prayer requests and being diligent in prayer, and no one is more right or wrong than the other. The important thing is that we make an effort to pray consistently.

If we want to tell our children that we've prayed for them, we need to be intentional about implementing prayer into our schedule. If you are more of a free spirit and less of a planner, you might simply pray for each child as you fall asleep at night. It doesn't have to require a complicated system. In fact, the less involved and rigid your system is, the better. You'll be more likely to stick with it if it isn't overwhelming to you.

As you think about your personal prayer life—especially in regard to your prayers for your children—what do you think might help you become a more consistent pray-er? Think of one practical idea you can implement into your prayer routine.

TRAINING

We certainly spend a lot of time teaching our children how to put their clothes away, change the toilet paper roll, and say please and thank you. Teaching them to pray is even more important!

I began teaching my children to pray when they were very small, but as they grew, I realized the need for more instruction in prayer when I began to notice repetition in their nightly prayers. For several nights in a row, they prayed, "Lord, I just thank you for this wonderful day today, and I pray we'd have a wonderful day tomorrow. Amen." So I decided to ask them if they had anything else they wanted to talk to God about. I noticed that if I made suggestions, they were very open to adding them, but they were reluctant to initiate deeper conversation with their Maker. So I concluded that perhaps they needed intentional training in prayer.

The truth is, all of our children need intentional training in prayer. Other than teaching them simple prayers they can memorize and recite, which is often what we do with very young children, what might intentional training in prayer look like?

1. We can follow Jesus's example when teaching our children to pray.

Though Jesus modeled prayer, he also gave his disciples some practical training in how to do it. Both Matthew and Luke record a teachable moment when Jesus told his disciples how to pray.

In Matthew 6, Jesus initiates the lesson by teaching them what prayer is not. Basically, he tells them:

- Don't pray publicly just so you can be seen by others and thought spiritual (v. 5).
- Don't babble on, repeating the same words over and over (v. 7).

In Luke's Gospel, the disciples say to Jesus, "Lord, teach us to pray, just as John taught his disciples" (11:1b). In each account, Jesus then teaches them the Lord's Prayer. In Matthew 6, it reads like this:

Our Father in heaven,
>may your name be kept holy.
May your Kingdom come soon.
May your will be done on earth,
>as it is in heaven.
Give us today the food we need,
and forgive us our sins,
>as we have forgiven those who sin against us.
And don't let us yield to temptation,
>but rescue us from the evil one. (Matthew 6:9-13)

Jesus didn't intend for them merely to repeat these words over and over. In fact, he had just warned them not to babble on and on, repeating the same words as the pagans did. Instead, he was teaching them some basic elements that should be included in our dialogues with our gracious and loving God. The acrostic ACTS captures these elements. It stands for the following: **A**doration, **C**onfession, **T**hanksgiving, **S**upplication.

These were big words at the time for my then five-year-old daughter, eight-year-old twin daughters, and eleven-year-old son. So I asked God to help me teach them to pray in a way that would go deeper than their surface prayers for a good day without being insincere, fancy words they simply repeated with little understanding.

A Practical Approach: Teaching ACTS

Here's how I broke down the acronym ACTS for my kids:

Adoration

Sometimes my children could be silly when we closed our eyes to pray. Though I didn't want them to think that God and prayer aren't fun, I did want them to know that when we get quiet to pray, we need to remember that God is holy—which means "set apart." When we talk to God, we need to remember we are addressing the God of the universe and praise him for who he is.

I thought about how my children could praise God each day in a way that wouldn't get rote or mechanical. I got a piece of construction paper, and we spent one night brainstorming words that describe God, such as *powerful, loving, awesome, holy*. They had fun coming up with these words. Then I asked them some of the names for God found in the Bible. With a little coaxing, they thought of *rock, shepherd, Jesus, King of kings*. Soon we had filled the page with different ideas. I bought a cute white frame and hung up the list in their room. At bedtime they could each pick one of the things on the list to begin their prayer.

Confession

This part turned out to be the most surprising. The first time we talked about confession, none of them could recall any bad thing they had done that day. I was floored. I had a long list for each of them fresh on my mind! I held back as long as I could, but then I asked one of them, "What about hitting your sister today?"

"Oh, yeah."

Then on to the next child: "Remember how you threw that fit and got in trouble this morning?"

"I had forgotten about that."

They were all very willing to confess their sins to God and were even excited that they had something for this part of the prayer. They just needed some training and direction.

Thanksgiving

Giving thanks came more naturally. They were always grateful for the "wonderful day." Now we tried to be more specific. What are we thankful for? Yes, we had trips to the park, friends over, and new toys. But we talked about some basic things that we often take for granted: freedom to worship, our own copy of God's Word, clean water, food, eyes to see, legs to run. Their tender hearts were telling their Creator that they had much to appreciate. Children don't always remember these blessings in day-to-day life when surrounded by ads and commercials tempting them to want more. But at night when their hearts are soft, they often recognize God's provision when a loving parent reminds them of all he has done.

Supplication

Big word. I told them we were basically just asking God for things. He invites us to ask with shameless persistence. We can ask for things we need or want, but we also want to pray for others. A friend of mine shared a great system that she used to help her kids remember what they were praying for each day. We made another poster for the wall that looked like this:

Monday: Missionaries. Here we wrote the name of two specific families we know and support. We prayed for their children and tried to remember to share any details about their families we received in regular prayer updates in e-mails or letters.

Tuesday: Teachers. Each child prayed for his or her own school teacher. We also listed the names of their piano teacher, Sunday school teachers, and coaches. If they didn't know what to pray, we asked God to give their teachers wisdom and endurance. (They can always use a little more of that, right?)

Wednesday: Widows and orphans. We prayed for specific ones we knew. We prayed for Great-Grandma, a woman at church, and for little Alex and Robelina, whom we support through an organization that provides opportunities to sponsor needy children. (Our son and the twins have since been able meet Alex personally on mission trips to Guatemala. It was incredible for them to meet the boy we had prayed for on so many Wednesdays.)

Thursday: Those who don't have a relationship with Jesus. The children had plenty of people who were school friends, neighbors, or extended family members whom they hope will accept Jesus's gift of salvation and choose to follow him. It made the celebration that much sweeter when we saw a family we had been praying for in our neighborhood place their faith in Christ.

Friday: Friends and family. We listed all the cousins, aunts and uncles, and grandparents, and each child picked one or two special friends to include. Living in Ohio with my family in Texas and my husband's family in Canada, praying for family helps my kids feel more connected with people they may get to see only once a year.

After we implemented our new approach to prayer, we found that our kids' prayer lives were growing stronger. It hasn't been a perfect system. Still, the kids have learned that prayer is talking with God about anything and everything. They have practiced remembering who he is, where they fall short, and what they are thankful for, and they have asked for God's help for others. Though we no longer have the lists on the wall, they have long since moved past talking generically about a "wonderful day" to deeper connection with Christ. (We're still working on that toilet paper roll, though!)

2. We can invest our time and creativity in teaching our children to pray.

Whether God leads you to implement the ACTS approach to teaching your child to pray or another practical method, it's important to give both your time and creativity as you model and train in the importance of prayer. Without prayer, we drift away from God just as we do from friends we rarely talk to anymore. We don't want our children to just know about God; we want them to have a close relationship with him.

Spend some time now asking God this question: What approach would you like me to take in teaching my children about prayer? Channel some of the creativity energy you typically expend on decorating their rooms or finding the right birthday party favors to coming up with some engaging ideas to teach them about prayer. Maybe you could start a Pinterest board of prayer ideas that you find. Many of our family prayer ideas were short lived. We implemented them for only a few months or possibly even a year. Yet I'm glad we did each and every one and wish we had attempted even more. Don't wait until you find the perfect system, and don't be discouraged if it dies out with time and life transitions. Celebrate what you did for even a short amount of time.

A Practical Approach: Other Prayer Ideas

Here are some other practical prayer ideas we've used for different seasons in our family:

- Put all of the Christmas cards/pictures received in a basket. Have a child draw one at dinner and pray for the family.
- Use a story from the book *Window on the World: When We Pray God Works* (Daphne Spraggett and Jill Johnstone, [Downer's Grove, IL: IVP Books, 2007]) to learn about different countries and assign one prayer need from the list to each child during mealtime (great for widows and orphans on Wednesday). The website www.reachthepoorthisweek.com, which lists a story of a real child in a developing country and gives prayer requests, is another great resource.
- Make journals and let every child write down prayer requests.
- Get in the living room and let every child take a different posture during prayer time (lying down, kneeling, standing). Teach them that they can pray in any position and at any time.
- Pray immediately when something bad happens.

That last idea brings back a wonderful memory. One day we gathered and prayed for God to return our bird, Monty, that had escaped from the cage. Of course, I remembered to add, "If it is God's will for him to be in our family." Monty did come back after several days of the neighbors letting us know his movements around the street. The yellow Conure stood out with his bright color and shrill shriek. I'll never forget my children's heartfelt prayers and excitement when he came back. (Although, truthfully, I could have easily accepted that it wasn't God's will for Monty to be a Spoelstra.)

We certainly didn't always follow through with all of our prayer plans; busy schedules often got in the way of consistency. Yet we never stopped talking about prayer and trying new things to make prayer a priority in our home. As you spend time talking to the Lord, I hope you'll be inspired to pursue teaching your child with all your creative energy. When your child has a specific need or a question about prayer, you'll be ready to answer through modeling and training. Take a few moments right now to pray Paul's prayer for the Ephesian believers on behalf of your child or children:

> When I think of all this, I fall to my knees and pray to the Father, the Creator of everything in heaven and on earth. I pray that from his glorious, unlimited resources he will empower you with inner strength through his Spirit. Then Christ will make his home in your hearts as you trust in him. Your roots will grow down into God's love and keep you strong. And may you have the power to understand, as all God's people should, how wide, how long, how high, and how deep his love is. May you experience the love of Christ, though it is too great to understand fully. Then you will be made complete with all the fullness of life and power that comes from God. Now all glory to God, who is able, through his mighty power at work within us, to accomplish infinitely more than we might ask or think. Glory to him in the church and in Christ Jesus through all generations forever and ever! Amen. (Ephesians 3:14-21)

Discussion Topics

Group Discussion Questions

- Who taught you to pray? When and how did they do it?

- What kinds of questions about prayer have your children asked?

- Jesus intentionally leveraged time away from people and tasks to spend time in prayer. What are some people and things you may need to give yourself permission to withdraw from in order to make prayer a priority in your own life?

- What are some ways you have organized daily and weekly prayer requests to help you stay consistent in prayer?

- What have been some of your most memorable teachable moments with your kids related to prayer?

Getting into God's Word

- Look up Matthew 6:5-13 and read it together. What about Jesus's teaching on prayer challenges you to make changes in your own times of prayer?

- Look up John 17 and read the chapter together. How does Jesus's prayer reveal the depth of his relationship with the Father and his desire for us to know him too?

- Which one of these principles from Jesus's prayer life resonates most with you right now?

1. Jesus intentionally pulled away from other responsibilities to spend time alone with the Father.

2. Jesus communicated to his disciples that he was praying for them.

3. Jesus taught us to pray in faith.

4. Jesus prayed out loud in front of people to build their faith.

5. Jesus prayed for God's will over his own.

- What is one new practical approach you would like to take in training your child or children to pray?

Digging Deeper

- Read aloud as a group some of the great prayers recorded in Scripture that are listed below. Look for any elements of Adoration, Confession, Thanksgiving, and Supplication in these prayers.

  o Daniel's Prayer: Daniel 9:1-19

  o Habakkuk's Prayer: Habakkuk 3

  o Jehoshaphat's Prayer: 2 Chronicles 20:5-12

  o Hezekiah's Prayer: 2 Kings 19:15-19

  o Mary's Prayer: Luke 1:46-55

- Discuss how these prayers challenge you in your own personal time alone with God.

CHAPTER 2
READING GOD'S WORD

We had an epic fail the first time we tried to have family devotions with our kids. It was during the holiday season, and we were overly eager to make Christmas more about Jesus than other characters that get a lot of holiday press. We made ornaments that went along with a Bible reading plan for each day in December. This particular guide also gave corresponding pages to the stories in a beginner Bible that had pictures and easy-to-understand language. We thought it might work even though the twins were barely two years old.

On the first night, the lesson was about how God created the world. My husband, Sean, had patiently made it through the whole lesson despite lots of squirming and distracting twin-isms, and he was reviewing by asking a few questions. Our five-year-old son, Zach, had been joyfully participating and was eager to answer all the questions. Sean asked Zach to let Sara and Abby answer his last simple question: "Who made the world?" Jubilantly Sara said, "I did it! I made the world!" My husband chuckled and then said, "No, really. Who made the world?" Now she was doubting herself and said with a questioning tone in her voice, "Mommy did it?"

We still laugh about this, and thankfully I captured it all on video! Though it wasn't the best theological moment in our home, we learned not to push toddlers along too far and too fast. It's important to consider children's ages and attention spans when it comes to exploring God's Word. As parents, we want our kids to know and love our amazing God, not dread what they perceive to be "lecture time." Our hope is that they will learn to look to God's Word for the answers to life's questions because it is the source of truth.

As I've sought to follow God, His Word has been the vehicle he has used most frequently to reveal himself to me. I don't worship the Bible, but I follow the God of the Bible. Reading and studying God's Word is like daily spiritual food. So if I want my children to grow into fully developed followers of Christ, then I must teach them how to eat the spiritual food of Scripture.

When my kids were babies, I breastfed them and eventually fed them baby food. The first three loved to eat, but my youngest was quite resistant to any type of nourishment. Doctors labeled Rachel with the term "failure to thrive" after six months of steadily moving down the growth chart. She was born in the fiftieth percentile for weight. At two months she had fallen to the twenty-fifth percentile. At four months she hovered in the tenth percentile, and by six months old the line on her growth chart had moved to the third percentile. My pediatrician said there is nothing wrong with being in the third percentile if you hold that line. It was her steady decline that concerned him.

You can imagine the frustration this caused her momma! I wanted her to eat so she could grow. Feeding her became my mission. I quit nursing her so we could measure how much she ate. She refused every bottle nipple available. Even when she finally would drink out of a bottle, she never took more than two ounces at one time. High-chair time was even worse. She would clench her jaw and close her lips when I tried to spoon food into her mouth. My pediatrician said to persist in putting her in the high chair three times a day, and eventually my husband and I would wear her down. It was a battle of wills daily. One time my sweet husband offered to take over. He tried patiently for several minutes and encountered the same closed lips and shaking of the head. The next feeding time he said in exasperation, "Let's just put it all over her face and bib and say we did it. That's all that happens anyway!" But after two solid weeks of food wars, she finally relented and started to eat.

I remember thinking through the ordeal, "Wow, I wonder if this is how much God wants us to grow spiritually." When it comes to helping our children eat spiritual food, sometimes they embrace God's Word quickly. Other times we encounter more frustration and need perseverance to keep trying. In either case we begin by feeding them—spooning God's Word to them—but eventually we want them to learn to eat without our assistance. The writer of Hebrews used this same illustration: "You have been believers so long now that you ought to be teaching others. Instead, you need someone to teach you again the basic things about God's word. You are like babies who need milk and cannot eat solid food" (Hebrews 5:12). Just as we want to teach our babies to grow up and feed themselves physically, so we want to help them learn to study and apply God's Word so they can grow spiritually.

Let's read a few passages from Scripture that remind us why it's so important to teach our children to look to the Scriptures for answers:

> For the word of God is alive and powerful. It is sharper than the sharpest two-edged sword, cutting between soul and spirit, between joint and marrow. It exposes our innermost thoughts and desires. (Hebrews 4:12)

> All Scripture is inspired by God and is useful to teach us what is true and to make us realize what is wrong in our lives. It corrects us when we are wrong and teaches us to do what is right. God uses it to prepare and equip his people to do every good work. (2 Timothy 3:16-17)

> Your word is a lamp to guide my feet
>   and a light for my path. (Psalm 119:105)

> The grass withers and the flowers fade,
>   but the word of our God stands forever. (Isaiah 40:8)

According to these four short passages, we find that the Bible

- is alive and powerful;
- exposes our innermost thoughts and desires;
- is inspired by God;
- teaches us what is true;
- shows us what is wrong in our lives;
- corrects us when we are wrong;
- instructs us to do what is right;
- prepares and equips us to do every good work;
- guides our feet and lights our path;
- stands forever

That's the kind of book I want my children to be well versed in! I want them to realize and experience the power of God's Word in their lives.

To help our children mature in faith, we must teach them to cling to this book that is full of truth and power. It will be the source and authority we rely on as we approach spiritual modeling and training. We can show our children that we aren't making up the rules about life and godliness; we are just trying to follow God.

So where do we start?

MODELING

Let's look again to the life of Jesus to see how he modeled the importance of the Scriptures.

1. Jesus studied the Word of God, asking questions and growing in wisdom.

When Jesus was twelve, his parents couldn't find him as they were returning home from a trip to Jerusalem. We read in the Gospel of Luke, "When they couldn't find him, they went back to Jerusalem to search for him there. Three days later they finally discovered him in the Temple, sitting among the religious teachers, listening to them and asking questions. All who heard him were amazed at his understanding and his answers" (2:45-47). We see that Jesus listened and asked questions even as a child. Jesus was God's Son, and as a child he modeled for us how to approach the Scriptures.

My niece and I have a great fondness for Curious George books. That funny little monkey is always getting into trouble because of his inquisitive nature. One story is about Curious George and the lost puppy. When George and the man with the yellow hat visit a kennel, one of the puppies is missing. George gets curious as everyone is looking for the puppy and fiddles with the cages. He accidently lets out all the puppies, causing chaos. But as they round up the animals, one of the dogs finds the lost puppy. In the end, everyone gets back where they need to be, and George's curiosity solves the ultimate problem—even though it causes some initial mayhem.

Likewise, asking good questions and listening to different viewpoints can rattle some cages in our lives. As we study and learn, we may find some beliefs that we held tightly need a looser grip. Other things we didn't hold tightly we might discover are near to God's heart.

My Bible's margins are filled with question marks, because I often struggle to understand things in God's Word. Whenever I am puzzled about God's Word, I remember 1 Corinthians 13:12, which confirms that our current understanding is incomplete: "Now we see things imperfectly, like puzzling reflections in a mirror, but then we will see everything with perfect clarity. All that I know now is partial and incomplete, but then I will know everything completely, just as God now knows me completely."

Although our picture isn't complete, it is important to ask good questions and seek answers diligently. When you come across a passage of Scripture that is confusing, consider consulting commentaries from authors with varying viewpoints or asking a pastor or spiritual mentor to help you understand the passage. In Acts 17:11 we read that the people of Berea heard the message of the gospel, and "they searched the Scriptures day after day to see if Paul and Silas were teaching the truth."

When reading the Bible, we could do a little more searching, digging, and asking questions, but we must also be okay with some measure of ambiguity in our study of God's Word. Trying to tack everything down can lead us to dangerous places where we think we hold all the right answers on every verse. Some things are clear and we never should back down (such as the gospel message); other things are gray areas that we hold loosely, realizing that we see in a mirror dimly right now (such as worship styles and understandings of end times). If we aren't careful, we might find ourselves trying to do what Solomon warned us about—attempting to straighten God out (Ecclesiastes 7:14). We often want to force everything into black-and-white categories, but we must learn to live with some things in the gray areas when Scripture is not absolutely clear.

As we seek to answer our children's questions about God's Word, sometimes we will have to be okay with saying, "I don't know" or "Let's study that together." If God's Word isn't clear, then we can offer a few ideas or our own personal opinion, or we can tell our kids that we have lots of unanswered questions that we will ask Jesus when we meet him face to face. Until then, we continue to seek God diligently even in the midst of our questions.

If we want our children to approach God's Word with wonder and expectation, we could stand to practice more curiosity in our own study of the Bible.

- How do you approach God's Word as you study it personally? Do you ask questions and listen to others you respect? Do you take the time to dig deep and study when you don't understand something?
- In what ways would you like to become more like Curious George as you approach God's Word?

Jesus asked questions and listened as he studied God's Word. He also was clear about whom we are to look for in the Scriptures.

2. Jesus said that Scripture points us to him.

Jesus fulfilled the writings of the prophets. In the Scriptures, we discover who Jesus was and is.

You search the Scriptures because you think they give you eternal life. But the Scriptures point to me! (John 5:39)

Then Jesus said to them, "You foolish people! You find it so hard to believe all that the prophets wrote in the Scriptures. Wasn't it clearly predicted that the Messiah would have to suffer all these things before entering his glory?" Then Jesus took them through the writings of Moses and all the prophets, explaining from all the Scriptures the things concerning himself. (Luke 24:25-27)

In the beginning the Word already existed.
The Word was with God,
and the Word was God. (John 1:1)

For the essence of prophecy is to give a clear witness for Jesus. (Revelation 19:10b)

He wore a robe dipped in blood, and his title was the Word of God. (Revelation 19:13)

From these passages we find that the Scriptures point to Jesus as the Messiah. He was and is the Living Word of God. So as we study Scripture, we should be looking for a clear witness of Jesus.

We must guard against becoming like the Pharisees, who immersed themselves in the Scriptures but missed the heart of God. They got caught up in rules over relationship. As we seek to model the proper use of Scripture, we want our kids to see us looking for Jesus in God's Word.

I must confess that at times I have been a Scripture bully with my kids. I can wield a verse about laziness or obedience to shame them or motivate them to comply. It isn't an effective pursuit. Ephesians 6:17 tells us that the

Word of God is the sword of the Spirit, but it is a weapon to be used against our enemy the devil, not against other believers and certainly not against our children.

We have one child who really struggled with anger from a young age. When nothing seemed to help with her fits and outbursts of emotion (which she came by very honestly from both her parents), we tried an anger worksheet that we had read about somewhere. Basically, we set up a little place where she had to go when she had a fit, and she couldn't leave until she filled out a sheet that asked what had made her angry and how she could have responded differently, and that asked her to look up and write out a Bible verse. While this sounds good in theory, she usually ripped up the first worksheet and needed another one when she was calmer. One day she ripped up some pages from the Bible that we provided to help her find a Bible verse to write on the worksheet. I remember heading down to our basement and crying out to God, "What have we done wrong? My daughter is ripping up your Word!"

Have you been there? Maybe your child hasn't ripped up the Bible but has expressed an attitude toward it that breaks your heart. Whether it's anger or neglect they express, the way to help our children value the Bible is not to use it punitively. My daughter didn't need a Bible verse in her moments of rage. She needed time to calm down. Clearly our plan didn't grow her love for God's Word. It became part of a punishment. Through our many failures in parenting, I've learned not to use the Bible in a disciplinary way with our children. I want them to see it as the Word of Life that shows us Jesus.

Jesus is the living Word of God, and he takes our punishment on himself. He rescues rather than condemns. He said to the woman caught in adultery: "'Where are your accusers? Didn't even one of them condemn you?' 'No, Lord,' she said. And Jesus said, 'Neither do I. Go and sin no more'" (John 8:10-11). We also find these powerful words in Romans 8:1: "There is no condemnation for those who belong to Christ Jesus."

Jesus called us to turn from our sin and toward God. He used the Scriptures to help people get to know the Father and expose truth. He gave grace to the humble and law to the proud. He did not use the Scriptures to manipulate or shame.

Making Scripture part of a punishment for a child might not be the best way to show them God's heart in it. Now we give our kids options that include memorizing verses or doing chores to earn special privileges or make amends. I believe the Word has power, and I want to motivate them to study and memorize it. But we should be careful how we model its use. It can be one option they can choose, but it should not be forced upon them as punishment.

So how can we be sure we are handling God's Word properly in our lives—in a way that points to Jesus?

One important principle we can learn from Jesus is to let the text speak. We have a tendency to read our own ideas into it. We can't make a decision about something and then go to the Bible to support what we have already concluded. That's called proof texting. If we aren't careful, we can twist the Bible to say anything we want it to say when we're looking to prove a point. We must lay aside our baggage when we open God's Word. Our childhood religious traditions, preconceived notions, and cultural ideas must all take a backseat to the clear reading of the text.

While some passages may contain poetry, allegory, or metaphors, we only utilize that interpretation when the text itself does so. For example, we know when Jesus said, "I am the gate," he was speaking of a spiritual gate, not a literal one. Rather than read into the text what we want it to say, we should look for God's heart, looking to study resources and asking the Spirit to give us wisdom in discerning his message.

We must let God's Word speak for itself without adding to, changing, or making something up so that it makes more sense in our finite brains. Moses sums it up in Deuteronomy 4:2 when he says, "Do not add to or subtract from these commands I am giving you. Just obey the commands of the LORD your God that I am giving you."

- As you seek to model for your child or children the importance of studying God's Word, what baggage do you need to lay aside?

- Do you tend to study Scripture looking for God's heart and relevant principles or for proof that the views you already hold are right?

Your words, attitudes, and conversations about God's Word will shape your child's relationship with God's Word. Ask God to help you see any unhealthy approaches to Scripture in your own life. For me, at times I value knowledge of history and facts and miss the simple but powerful and clear witness of Jesus. Jesus wants our time in the Bible to draw us nearer to him. I want that for my children as well, but it has to start with me.

- What is one practical change you can make in your devotional time to let the text speak to your heart in a fresh way?

3. Jesus taught the Scriptures with authority, revealing a depth of knowledge.

Jesus taught with authority. He said that those who build their lives on his teaching will have a strong foundation.

> "Anyone who listens to my teaching and follows it is wise, like a person who builds a house on solid rock. Though the rain comes in torrents and the floodwaters rise and the winds beat against that house, it won't collapse because it is built on bedrock. But anyone who hears my teaching and doesn't obey it is foolish, like a person who builds a house on sand. When the rains and floods come and the winds beat against that house, it will collapse with a mighty crash." When Jesus had finished saying these things, the crowds were amazed at his teaching, for he taught with real authority—quite unlike their teachers of religious law. (Matthew 7:24-29)

We want that kind of strong foundation for our kids, yet we can feel inadequate when it comes to God's Word:

- We fear we won't explain it right.
- We don't want to join a Bible study because others will think we are biblically illiterate.
- We assume everyone knows more about God's Word than we do.
- We don't know where in the Scriptures to go when our child has a question.

These statements are Satan's victories. Our God never condemns us. Condemnation draws us away from God, his Word, and other believers. The conviction of the Holy Spirit might prompt us to change, but it always draws us toward our gracious God.

When it comes to helping our children build a strong foundation on God's Word, we must not let the enemy win! We are so much more capable than we realize. God's Word is not so complicated that we can't understand it. No matter how little or how much we know, we can study to learn and grow. God has called us to be the key disciple-makers in our children's lives, so studying his Word should be a top priority.

Never before have we possessed such easy access to God's Word and great teachings that explain it. Though we are busy and juggle multiple balls, that is all the more reason we need time daily in God's Word—so we can keep all those balls in the air or at least know which ones it's okay to drop. We'll never do it perfectly, but one thing is certain: our time in God's Word should not be the priority we let fall.

We must not believe the lie that we cannot adequately understand, teach, or speak from God's Word with authority. Christ did, and we are following him, doing what he did. Though it can be hard to understand certain passages in the Bible, if we look for God's heart as we read and study, we will find it.

One dangerous trend I have noticed is the tendency to pick out one verse here and there, rather than reading the entire passage. While each verse of Scripture is true and many have great power when standing alone, we lose the depth of our foundation when we do not consider the context.

We live in a world of one-liners. Short quips, rather than well-developed thoughts, are modern fare. Social media is full of wise sayings and pithy statements, and blogs that highlight a few action points often win out over lengthier books. Our attention spans and those of our children have been swept away with the culture. As a result, we often isolate verses from the Bible without considering what comes before and after them.

In college, someone made a poster for our dorm that had pictures of male models and this verse: "Be merciful to me, O God, for men hotly pursue me" (Psalm 56:1a NIV 1984). Although it was a joke, this illustrates in an exaggerated way how we can twist Scripture for our own purposes. David wrote this particular psalm when King Saul's men were chasing him relentlessly and he was forced to hide in caves. Do you see how we (I mean other gals) took it out of context to skew its original intent?

When we know something about the author, the original audience, the historical backdrop, and the cultural norms, it helps us unwrap the underlying truth. We then take the correctly interpreted principle from God and reapply it in our own cultural context.

Here are some good questions to ask when trying to understand the meaning of a verse:

- How did the author intend this to be understood and why?
- Why did God include and preserve this in Scripture?
- What biblical principle is found here?
- How does this fit in with the whole of Scripture?
- What application does this truth have in our modern culture?

These questions help us with context. When I asked five respected leaders to share important interpretation principles when reading Scripture, all five included the word *context* in their top two. Context helps give us greater understanding. The Bible contains timeless truths, but sometimes our modern mind-set can trip us up when reading ancient texts. It doesn't take much extra effort to read more of a passage to find context. Sometimes we simply give up too easily.

I want to challenge you as you seek to model the importance of Scripture.

If you are already spending time in God's Word each day, that is great. I know many moms who use a daily Bible reading plan. I like to use the YouVersion app on my phone, and there are other wonderful apps as well. Other moms participate in a small group or Bible study with daily lessons that help them understand and apply God's Word. Many read a daily devotional to focus on one or two main truths from Scripture.

What about you?

- Do you already have a plan for daily time in God's Word?
- Do you hear God calling you to make any changes in your approach and method to God's Word?
- Are you spending the amount of time studying the Bible daily that you hope your children will spend when they grow up?

If you are already modeling the habit of reading and studying the Bible, I pray you will move even deeper in your pursuit of building a strong foundation on God's Word in your own life. I hope you will consider the following:

- listening and asking more questions
- letting the text speak
- looking for Jesus and the gospel message as you study
- gaining confidence to speak God's word with authority

Which one of these things might God be asking you to focus on in the coming weeks and months? Share your answer with another mom, and ask her if she would be willing to pray for you and check in with you periodically.

Now if you're saying, "Ugh. I don't have a plan. I try to read God's Word here and there, but it is not a regular part of my spiritual life," that's okay. No condemnation here! But I want to challenge you, because I know how hard it is to try to feed my kids when I'm starving myself. Even baby food can start to look appetizing when we are truly hungry! Trying to live as Christ-followers without the Word of God renewing and transforming our minds is beyond difficult.

So, I invite you to take this thirty-one-day challenge.

A Practical Approach: The Proverbs Thirty-One-Day Challenge

You can start today. It's that simple. Whatever day of the month it is, read that chapter in Proverbs today. Let me tell you why I find this such a great place to start for parents.

- Proverbs is packed full of parenting wisdom.
- There are thirty-one Proverbs and around thirty-one days each month.
- If you miss a day, it's easy to get back on track. You just look at the calendar for the day of the month and know exactly where to go. (You will probably miss a day here and there. Everybody does; we all are human. The key is to start again rather than get discouraged and quit.)
- Each chapter in Proverbs stands alone, so you can miss chapters without losing context.
- You will laugh, cry, and see God's heart in these words of wisdom.
- They say it takes twenty-eight days to make a habit, so at the end of the month you will be hooked on God's Word!

I hope that you will take me up on this! If you do and you are on social media, would you hash tag #Proverbschallenge so that we can encourage one another? This simple exercise can be life-changing!

- Which of the three principles we've explored strikes a chord of conviction in your study habits right now?
- Is there one practical change you can make today to deepen your time in God's Word?

- Will you take the Proverbs challenge—or some other Bible reading plan or app—this month so you can model the study habits you would like to see in your child?

Now let's move beyond modeling to the next step, which is training our children in the habit of reading and studying the Bible.

TRAINING

Recently my eighteen-year-old son got a ticket on his car while it was parked on our street because his registration tags were expired. He was so confused. Sean and I have modeled the act of getting new tags every year for our vehicles, but we did a poor job in training our son. He didn't even realize what we were doing all those years. I had given him the paper telling him to take care of it, but I never instructed him, followed up, or mentioned the consequences of not registering. I modeled well but trained poorly.

When it comes to instilling a love for God's Word in our children, we must do more than just provide an example. We hope our kids will find us reading our Bibles, listening to the Bible on our phones, or working on our Bible study lessons. Yet often we do those things while they are sleeping, playing, or focused on television or a handheld device. They may or may not even notice. We must go a step further and train our kids to study Scripture.

There is a difference between feeding our children and teaching them to feed themselves. Though training begins with feeding them Scripture, the ultimate goal is to equip them to read and study the Bible on their own. Specific challenges include age and developmental learning abilities as well as each child's unique personality, birth order, and spiritual interest level. Other considerations are time and distractions. With busy schedules and short attention spans, we must be intentional and creative with both planned and unplanned instruction and activities—finding ways to help our children discover the goodness of God's Word for themselves. Let's explore these challenges.

1. Being Sensitive to Age and Developmental Abilities

Just as our attempt to do family devotions with our two-year-old twins didn't go well, we must be careful not to have unrealistic expectations about what our kids are able to do at a particular age. This means we have to get creative and out of our comfort zones to help our children learn to study God's Word in meaningful ways appropriate to their ages and development.

When we ask a kindergartener to read from a Bible that is written on a twelfth-grade reading level, we are setting everyone up for failure. We would do well to know the reading levels of various Scripture translations so that we may choose accordingly. Here is one helpful chart:

- King James Version: twelfth grade
- New American Standard Bible: eleventh grade
- English Standard Version: seventh to eighth grade
- Holman Christian Standard Bible: seventh to eighth grade
- New King James Version: seventh grade
- New Living Translation: sixth grade
- The Message: fourth to fifth grade
- Contemporary English Version: fourth grade
- New Century Version: third grade
- New International Reader's Version: third grade[1]

Christian bookstores and online resources (many of them free) can help us find age-appropriate Bibles, books, and activities to help our children devour God's Word.

2. Seizing Unplanned Teaching Times

In addition to being sensitive to age appropriateness, our training should include both unplanned and planned activities. Unplanned activities are those things that happen during unexpected moments. These are conversations we have with our children about a passage, story, or idea from Scripture while riding in the car, taking a nature walk, or responding to a difficult situation that arises. As Deuteronomy 6:6-7 tells us, "You must commit yourselves wholeheartedly to these commands that I am giving you today. Repeat them again and again to your children. Talk about them when you are at home and when you are on the road, when you are going to bed and when you are getting up."

Jesus did a lot of this unplanned teaching. He talked about what the Scriptures said about money, faith, heaven, and all sorts of other topics as he and the disciples completed mundane tasks such as walking along the road, reclining at meals, and attending weddings and funerals.

As God's Word comes alive in our own hearts, it will overflow into our conversations and daily rhythms. Travel time, play time, and even chore time can be opportunities for talking about God. Some sweet moments I've had with several of my kids have been when I've been working on memorizing some verses and I've asked them to check me on the wording. They love to correct me since I am usually the one pointing out their errors. It isn't planned or manipulative; I legitimately need some help because my memory verse partner has a photographic memory and is always way ahead of me! My competitive spirit can't stand to be behind, so I truly appreciate their help as I practice. While that motive may not be the best, the fruit of chatting with my kids about the passage is truly a treat.

Sometimes unplanned spiritual conversations can feel very inconvenient. When I'm tired or moody, it can be difficult to see the teachable moments. I often say jokingly that after nine at night, Jesus leaks right out of me. In the late evening I have to reorient my frame of thinking or I miss important times to listen and share in what God is doing in my kids' lives.

One of the greatest challenges for Sean and me has been that our kids seem to be most receptive to reading the Bible and talking about spiritual things at night when we are exhausted from the day. Too many times through the years we stopped short of a great training opportunity rather than take the extra five minutes it would require. Now my kids are teenagers, but thankfully they still want us to pray with them before bed. This is time when we can read a passage from the Bible and talk about it. Honestly, I usually don't feel like it because I'm tired; but when I push past my excuses and follow through, I find such sweet moments I wouldn't want to miss. Your child may be more open and receptive in the early morning, after school, or before or after dinner. The idea is to be ready and willing to take advantage of those valuable opportunities to teach them about God's Word—even when you have to "push through" to do it.

- Take a moment now to pray that God would give you eyes to see opportunities to bring his Word into everyday conversation.
- Can you think of a recent encounter with your child when you were able to dialogue about spiritual things at an unexpected time?

3. Planning Teaching Times

We will also want to plan times and ways to train our children in studying and applying Scripture in their lives. These plans will vary greatly depending on their ages and personalities. Here are some ideas we've used with our kids through the years. Perhaps they will spark ideas of your own.

A Practical Approach: Getting into God's Word Together

When our children were small we:

- did object lessons out of a book at the dinner table once a week (using toothpicks, toothpaste, and other tactile stuff so they didn't get bored).
- used the material from a weekly church program that included age appropriate ideas.

- listened to CDs in the car that told kid-friendly stories with second-level humor we all enjoyed. (OK, maybe we still do this while they are in high school; we are addicted to Adventures in Odyssey!)
- tried lots of different "family devotion" plans and failed. (It worked best when we kept it short and fun and included ice cream.)
- read a story each night from an age-appropriate Bible with lots of pictures.

As they have gotten older, we have:

- had family meetings occasionally to address problems, pray for one another, read a devotion, and eat fried chicken on the living room floor on a picnic blanket.
- bought them age-appropriate devotionals and showed them Bible apps on their phones, encouraging them to spend time with God and to journal.
- read through books of the Bible together, covering a little each night before bedtime.
- asked them lots of questions about whatever they are learning at church or youth group (to the point that they sometimes dread the car ride home).
- sent them to church activities and camps where we knew God's Word would be taught in relevant and age-appropriate ways.

This is definitely a place where we must leave the parenting report card behind. My own kids have had very different reactions to our attempts to train them in learning to study and apply God's Word on their own. Our son's personality type lends itself toward structure and self-discipline. He started a daily reading plan in the Bible as a third-grader and has basically had some kind of plan ever since. Even through high school he would come upstairs to use our bathroom in the mornings while listening to the Bible on his phone. He has had many different books and plans, but we don't feed him God's Word anymore. Praise God, he has learned to feed himself.

Now, don't give me a parenting grade! Not all of my kids have embraced daily time in God's Word so easily or readily. In fact, some have struggled to study the Bible on their own. They have tried lots of things but have not found anything that really sticks for long. In other areas of their lives—such as chores, neatness, and exercise—they also find self-discipline tough. But they are very strong in areas of compassion, relationships, and passion for God. While my son has less trouble with spiritual disciplines, some of the latter don't come naturally for him.

Just as I don't want a parenting grade based on my kids' choices at any given time, we can't evaluate our children's spiritual temperature based solely on whether they have developed a daily routine of time in God's Word. It is only one piece of a very complicated puzzle that God alone can see.

Looking at our children's spiritual lives can sometimes feel like having half of a completed puzzle without the box top. We can't see the end result. We get glimpses of what is going on, but God alone sees the finished product. We must be careful not to make judgments based on one or two factors. Even so, just as we know we must teach our children to make healthy food choices, so we must be intentional in training our children to feed themselves spiritually—and this takes time and persistence. At this point, Sean and I know that we must read the Bible with some of our kids if we want to make sure they get fed.

4. Being Careful About Soul Junk Food

Not only do I want to be sure my children feed their spirits but also I want to be careful about soul junk food. If I were to lay out apples and cookies for my kids, I know which one they would devour first! In our media-driven world, my kids have access to the Bible on their handheld devices, but they also have a world of soul junk food at their fingertips. Sometimes when I'm struggling in parenting, I think about how much media they consume and how little Bible they eat. It's tough for our little ones who are used to an entertainment industry that spends billions to make things exciting for them. We shouldn't be too shocked when they aren't thrilled to sit down with their Bible and hear from God. They are used to being spoon-fed candy, and we want to teach them to eat salad.

Before we throw up our hands and say the battle is uphill so why even try, let's remind ourselves that it *is* worth our effort. Remember the truths we read earlier about God's Word? It's alive, powerful, and transformative. We can't mandate spiritual disciplines in our children, but we can help them see the great truths and benefits that we find from studying God's Word.

Psalm 34:8 says, "Taste and see that the LORD is good. / Oh, the joys of those who take refuge in him!" We must keep setting the food out and encouraging our children to eat, hoping that eventually they will want it for themselves. When Ezekiel was instructed to eat the Word of God, he found it tasty: "The voice said to me, 'Son of man, eat what I am giving you—eat this scroll! Then go and give its message to the people of Israel.' So I opened my mouth, and he fed me the scroll. 'Fill your stomach with this,' he said. And when I ate it, it tasted as sweet as honey in my mouth" (Ezekiel 3:1-3).

- What are some ways you have attempted to help your child learn to read and study God's Word?
- What are some new ways you can help your child "taste and see" the goodness of God's Word?
- As you think about all the voices speaking into your child's soul through screens and speakers, what would you like to change so that these voices do not interfere with them understanding the power of God's Word?

A Practical Approach: Daily Application

If we want our children to taste and see the goodness of God, we can start with sharing what he is teaching us through his Word. Identify one truth or concept from your daily time in the Bible (whether you are taking the Proverbs Thirty-One-Day Challenge this month or have a different reading and study plan). Write this truth in your phone or on a note card, or underline it in your Bible. Then at bedtime, whether your child is six months or sixteen years old, share the truth with him or her—along with why it stood out to you or how you plan to apply it to your life. Keep it short and simple. I've found that the more elaborate the plan I make, the more destined it is to fail.

Even parents of infants can begin this practice. While you rock your baby, talk out loud about how:

- too much talk leads to sin (Proverbs 10:19a)
- gossip separates the closest of friends (Proverbs 16:28b)
- a gentle answer turns away wrath (Proverbs 15:1)
- those who love their children care enough to discipline them (Proverbs 13:24b)

Regardless of your child's age, I encourage you to start this practice today!

Depending on your personality, upbringing, or confidence level, talking about spiritual things doesn't always come naturally. It might take some planning, effort, and the willingness to move beyond your comfort zone. Despite any awkwardness you feel the first time you try the daily application idea with your child, keep in mind that it will become easier. Sharing what God is teaching you through his Word will whet your child's appetite. It might take decades to see your child reach for the apple over the cookie, but remember that "nothing you do for the Lord is ever useless" (1 Corinthians 15:58b).

To help our children learn to study and apply God's Word at an early age is well worth laying aside our discomfort and excuses. We can start right at home when answering Christ's call to make disciples. Our kids are watching, listening, and taking in what we say—even if they claim they don't want it, roll their eyes, or do not apply it in their lives right away.

- Will you try the daily application practice for the next thirty-one days, sharing each day with your child one truth from the Bible that God is teaching you?
- What excuses or challenges come to mind as to why this won't work for you?
- How can you overcome these obstacles and put feet to your desire to both model and train your children in the habit of making God's Word a priority?

While we will probably miss a day or two, fumble over our words, or possibly face a less than enthusiastic reaction from our children, we can become intentional and focused in our efforts. Remember that if we aim for nothing, we will hit it every time. Let's aim for thirty-one days of sharing biblical truth with our children; and if at the end of the month we have shared twenty truths, that will be twenty more than last month, right?

〰〰〰

A Practical Approach: Three Questions

For those with upper elementary, middle, and high school kids.
As we teach our children to dig into God's Word, I have found it helpful to give them some direction as they read. These three questions can help them get more out of their Bible time:

- What do I learn about God?
- What do I learn about myself (or people in general)?
- Is there anything God is saying to me through this passage that relates to what is going on in my life right now?

These questions give direction and something to be looking for while reading. Consider buying your child a notebook or journal and writing these three questions on the first page. Then as your child reads a passage, he or she can answer the questions in the journal.

The first question will help your child learn about our loving, strong, forgiving, and sacrificial God as he or she records discoveries. In answering the second question, your child will begin to relate to people in the Bible who made mistakes just as he or she does. I'm always encouraged to find that God continues to use messed-up people to accomplish amazing things for his kingdom. Finally, the last question will help your child begin making connections between God's Word and what he or she is experiencing.

So, even when you have an epic fail as we did when trying to teach two-year-olds who created the world, just keep trying. Those girls definitely aren't confused anymore, thinking I created the world. As teenagers they don't even think I can create a dinner that everyone will like! With perseverance and intentionality, we can model and train the value of seeking God through his Word. Even though we will never do it perfectly, we press on to help our kids embrace and understand the importance of the Bible as spiritual food that helps us grow in faith. And the hopeful part is that God's Word never comes back void or empty:

> The rain and snow come down from the heavens
> and stay on the ground to water the earth.
> They cause the grain to grow,
> producing seed for the farmer

and bread for the hungry.
It is the same with my word.
I send it out, and it always produces fruit.
It will accomplish all I want it to,
and it will prosper everywhere I send it. (Isaiah
55:10-11)

Keep sowing the seeds of God's Word in your child's heart, believing with confidence that even on the toughest of days, God will use it to accomplish all he wants. Everything may not come to fruition on our timetable or in a way that makes sense to us, but we can rest assured that time spent teaching our children to know and love the Bible is never wasted!

DISCUSSION TOPICS

Group Discussion Questions

- At what age did you receive your first Bible? Who gave it to you?

- Who taught you to study the Bible? What kind of instructions did they give you?

- What has helped you stay consistent in studying God's Word through different seasons of your Christian walk?

- How has God's Word helped you grow in faith?

- What have been the biggest inhibitors to teaching your child to study the Bible?

- What is one practical way you plan to be intentional in helping your child "taste and see" that God's Word is good?

Getting into God's Word

- Read aloud these verses from pages 29–30: Hebrews 4:12; 2 Timothy 3:16-17; Psalm 119:105; Isaiah 40:8. What truth about God's Word from these verses especially encourages you right now?

- Which of these truths that we studied from Jesus's life resonated with you and why?

  1. Jesus studied the Word of God, asking questions and growing in wisdom (Luke 2:45-46).

2. Jesus said that Scripture points us to him (John 5:39; Luke 24:25-27; John 1:1; Revelation 19:10b, 13).

3. Jesus taught the Scriptures with authority, revealing a depth of knowledge (Matthew 7:24-29).

- Do you have a life verse from Scripture—or a verse that has particular meaning for you? Share it with the group, explaining how it has brought you clarity or comfort.

Digging Deeper

- According to Psalm 19:7-11, what are some of the qualities and benefits of God's Word? How have these verses rung true in your own life?

- Read Psalm 119:9-16. What are some of the practical applications of God's truth in real life, according to the psalmist? How could these applications help your child as he or she grows in faith?

- Read John 8:31-32. What did Jesus say his teachings would bring us? How has truth brought freedom in your own life?

- Of all that we've studied about God's Word in this chapter, what stands out to you most?

CHAPTER 3

GROWING THROUGH MENTORING

When I had my first child, I had no clue what I was doing. My parents were doing ministry work in Albania at the time, so they couldn't be present to guide me. While I read some books and knew a few women at my church, I didn't feel close enough to ask practical newborn questions. We lived in a small town along the Georgian Bay in Ontario, Canada, which we found out later is the seventh snowiest city in all of North America. This Texas gal felt pretty isolated with all that snow in the months after my son was born in December!

For fear my son would experience nipple confusion, we didn't bring a pacifier to the hospital. Of course after he was born all he wanted to do was suck on something. My husband let him use his pinkie finger to keep him content. I began doing the same. I stood over that crib every night with my finger in his mouth! I was sleep deprived and knew there had to be a better way to get this kid to sleep. We tried the pacifier, but he had gotten used to fleshy warm fingers and wanted nothing to do with cold latex.

This was just one of the many things I look back on and chuckle. How I wish I'd had a mentor then—someone I could talk to for advice about diaper rash, sleep training, and the changes in marriage a baby brings. I'm so grateful that when we moved to Ohio eighteen months later, God graciously put an amazing mentor in my life.

Deb and I served together in youth ministry. She invited our family over for dinner and sometimes out to eat after church on Sundays. She didn't formally say, "Hey, can I be your mentor?" I didn't formally ask her either. Yet she became the person I called with parenting and marriage questions. When my five-year-old daughter had to be admitted into the ICU and put on a ventilator, Deb was my first call after my husband. She sat with me for hours day after day, praying with me and bringing me food. Just this week I got stuck on a parenting problem and dialed her number as I have so many times before.

Through the years I've had a front-row seat to how Deb handles her own parenting situations. She isn't perfect, but she is the mom I want to be. In the early days when we invited her family over for dinner, her older kids would play with our little ones so we actually could have a conversation. Her daughter has helped my girls through the teen years. As the years have passed, my husband and I have invested in her kids and even did her son's premarital counseling. I can tell you firsthand, for a parent seeking to follow Jesus, the benefits of a mentor are immeasurable.

Seeking a godly mentor is vital to the walk of faith—for us and our children. We need to show our children that we need a guide (modeling) and then also be intentional about mentoring our kids (training). Just by being their parents we're automatically their first advisors. But we also want them to learn to seek out wise counselors through every stage of their lives.

Thankfully, my children have been blessed to have mentors in their lives. Before leaving for college, my son met weekly with our young, fresh-out-of-college worship pastor who was married and five years older. They read books together, talked about life, and shared a common love for music as my son played drums on the worship team. I was grateful that he had, in addition to his dad and me, a reliable person to consult about dating and college and Jesus.

When the twins were freshmen in high school, two godly senior gals from their school took them under their wings. One girl invited Sara to her Bible study, then to a local campus ministry that followed. She drove my daughter to the meeting afterward and brought her home as well. That car time was valuable as they processed what they were learning. They met for coffee a few times to talk about life and faith. It meant the world to my daughter—and to her parents!

Abby also had a gal who drove her to youth group, invited her to a Bible study, and often asked her over for dinner with her family. I know most high school seniors prefer friends their own age, but these two amazing girls understood the importance of mentoring. They intentionally and relationally invested their time in girls younger than themselves.

My youngest, who is twelve, witnessed all this mentoring and did not want to be the only one without an adviser. She looked up to a sweet teen at our church and asked her to meet. This sixteen-year-old comes over and prays with my daughter, and they are working on a Bible study together.

These relationships are important because I know I am losing authority in their lives. In only a few short years they will all leave the nest (sniff, sniff). I pray they always have examples a little further down the spiritual road who are willing to be role models and take time to train them in godliness.

If we want our children to seek out mentors of their own, we can begin by modeling the value of having a mentor.

MODELING

Let's begin by defining what a mentor is. Merriam-Webster's says a mentor is "someone who teaches or gives help and advice to a less experienced and often younger person."[2]

As we realize how valuable it is to have someone to help and guide us, where do we start in finding one? We can have mentors in so many areas of life. At work we can have a coach who spurs us on to do our job better. At the gym we might hire a personal trainer to give us advice about how to work out more effectively. What we are talking about here, though, is a mentor who will guide us spiritually.

As you look at the parents around you, who would you say:

- spends time in God's Word and prayer regularly?
- treats those around them the way you want to treat others?
- parents their children the way you hope to—with patience and consistency?
- seems to have genuine spiritual connections with their kids?
- has a personality and sense of humor you enjoy?

Churches sometimes arrange mentoring relationships with mentees. But a natural connection that develops from personal contact, along with a commitment from both parties, is necessary for successful mentoring relationships. This isn't something you can force or program.

When I was in living in Canada as a young bride and my mom was living overseas, I tried to find a mentor. I had worked with several when I was a teen girl at my church, and I longed for that kind of spiritual support. I identified some role models and even initiated meeting regularly with one woman. When we met, though, the conversation never seemed to get beyond her garden and the weather. It wasn't what I had hoped it would be.

We might need to make several attempts before finding the right person. The whole process should be bathed in prayer. God says we can approach him for wisdom when we need it: "If you need wisdom, ask our generous God, and he will give it to you. He will not rebuke you for asking" (James 1:5).

When I moved to Ohio, I asked God to help me find some women who were older than I was who would be willing to guide me. I found that not only Deb but also the pastor's wife and another woman from church who led a Bible study for young moms quickly became resources for me in parenting and faith. Though Deb and I have never met regularly, we have shared life through vacations, graduations, health challenges, and birthday celebrations for over eighteen years.

Later when my husband felt called to plant a church, I got an opportunity to be coached by an experienced church-planter's wife. She lives two hours away, but we meet monthly using an online coaching tool and Skype. This mentoring is a little more structured, and she prepares questions ahead of time. In our hour together, she helps me celebrate where God is at work and tackle challenges in both my family and ministry.

We need to be strategic in pursuing a mentor but also realize our situation may look very different from another's mentoring relationship. If you do not currently have a mentor for spiritual guidance, who is someone you might seek out? When asking someone to be your mentor, you need to communicate what that means to you. When God brings someone to mind, consider the following issues before approaching the person:

- How often would you like to meet?
- What structure are you hoping for (informal talking, questions you go over each time, reading through a book, praying together, and so on)?
- Do your schedules allow for the time commitment you are seeking?
- Who will initiate making the connection?

I've heard many individuals complain that they asked someone to mentor them, but the person they asked never responded. I think that often a person being sought for mentoring is unclear what to do. Life is busy. Family time is demanding. You as the mentee should be clear about what kind of guidance you're looking for and be realistic about what you expect. And you should be able to articulate these issues to a potential mentor.

With Deb, I have no expectations. Since we both have family, work, and ministry commitments, weeks can go by without our talking. Because of her kindness, authenticity, and godly example, Deb also mentors many other women in our church. I don't feel territorial with her. When she meets with others or spoils their kids the way she does mine, I celebrate that others get to experience the joy I have in knowing her. I appreciate any time I get with Deb, but I don't expect her to be my Savior. I know she can't be omnipresent, perfectly wise, or the source of all truth. Besides, I already have a Savior—and he's amazing! I just count on Deb to help when and where she can.

I did seek out my church-planting coach and ask her to meet with me, even though it's via Skype. I knew she could guide me in ways that only someone who had been a church-planter's spouse could understand. Our meetings are much more structured and regular, and her guidance has been invaluable in helping me set and reach goals, find understanding and encouragement in ministry, and get advice about specific issues. But I do not expect her to celebrate my child's birthday with me. Our relationship is awesome, but different from the one I have with Deb.

※※※

A Practical Approach: Mentoring Questions

Jon and Dave Ferguson's book *Exponential* suggests six questions to guide mentors as they meet with their mentees[3]:

1. How are you?
2. What are you celebrating?
3. What challenges are you facing?
4. How will you tackle those challenges?
5. How can I help you?
6. How can I pray for you?

A structured dialogue built on these questions can provide a great framework, especially for initial meetings. Are there any questions you would add to these? You could give the list to a new mentor as an idea for your meetings. Remember that clear communication is one of the keys to the success of a great mentoring relationship.

※※※

As with any relationship, there are some of the pitfalls to guard against in mentoring. They include:

- lack of clear dialogue about expectations
- feeling territorial and wanting to be the only one your mentor helps

- personalities that don't naturally complement one another
- one person being more committed to the relationship than the other
- lack of margin in either party's life to make time for mentoring

If you have experienced a mentoring relationship that didn't turn out the way you expected, reflect on what might have contributed to the lack of success. Though that relationship was not what you had hoped for, don't give up—keep seeking a mentor who is right for you.

❧❧❧

A Practical Approach: Finding a Mentor

Here are some ideas for finding a mentor:

- Ask someone in your small group or Bible study to meet with you after class and discuss questions about your spiritual life.
- Look for a woman who is beyond the stage of parenting you are now in and ask if she'd be willing to meet you for lunch after church once a month.
- If a potential mentor is not in your local area, schedule regular one-hour online meetings with someone to discuss specific issues.
- Serve alongside a person you admire by joining him or her in ministry (Sunday school, youth ministry, hospitality, women's ministry).
- Ask your Bible study leader if you can be their apprentice/co-leader.
- Identify someone you look up to spiritually and use the mentoring questions on page 58 as a guide when meeting biweekly or monthly.

❧❧❧

Once we have found a spiritual coach or mentor for ourselves and established a plan for meeting, we must become purposeful with mentoring our own children. Of course our mentoring plan will change as our children develop and mature, but it's never too early or late to take a proactive approach in cultivating a mentoring relationship with each child.

TRAINING

When Jesus was a boy, Scripture says he "grew in wisdom and in stature and in favor with God and all the people" (Luke 2:52). His parents, Joseph and Mary, taught him many things. Jesus learned the trade of carpentry from his earthly father, Joseph, but ultimately God the Father was his greatest mentor. Years later Jesus explained, "I tell you the truth, the Son can do nothing by himself. He does only what he sees the Father doing. Whatever the Father does, the Son also does" (John 5:19). Jesus watched and emulated his heavenly Father just as our children have their eyes on us.

Jesus also modeled mentoring by picking twelve men to be his disciples. He invested in them by teaching them. We know from Scripture that he committed himself even more fully to three of them—Peter, James, and John. As we seek to mentor our own children in faith, we can learn from Christ's example.

1. Jesus engaged in spiritual conversations with his disciples.

Conversations require dialogue. This means talking and listening. Sometimes the disciples asked Jesus questions, and other times Jesus made inquiries of them. On one occasion, Jesus quoted from the prophet Jeremiah, saying, "These people honor me with their lips, / but their hearts are far from me. / Their worship is a farce, / for they teach man-made ideas as commands from God" (Matthew 15:8-9). The disciples asked Jesus, "Do you realize you offended the Pharisees by what you just said?" (Matthew 15:12b).

Jesus had been teaching a large group about not getting caught up with externals but instead focusing on inner purity. He took the time to explain his teaching and invited conversation about spiritual truth. Notice Jesus's response and how that opened the door for Peter to then ask more clarifying questions:

> Jesus replied, "Every plant not planted by my heavenly Father will be uprooted, so ignore them. They are blind guides leading the blind, and if one blind person guides another, they will both fall into a ditch." Then Peter said to Jesus, "Explain to us the parable that says people aren't defiled by what they eat." "Don't you understand yet?" Jesus asked. "Anything you eat passes through the stomach and then goes into the sewer. But the words you speak come from the heart—that's what defiles you. For from the heart come evil thoughts, murder, adultery, all sexual immorality, theft, lying, and slander. These are what defile you. Eating with unwashed hands will never defile you." (Matthew 15:13-20)

Jesus discipled his followers through constant dialogue. He welcomed questions without shaming the inquirers. He could have said, "Are you kidding me? Of course I know the Pharisees are offended!" Instead he used the opportunity to teach his followers and solicit more questions. The disciples' concerns over offending the Pharisees must have required Jesus's supernatural patience.

As we teach our children about their heavenly Father, we can

- learn to open the lines of communication by listening with understanding;
- encourage spiritual questions of any sort;
- choose not to be insulted when they assume we don't know things;
- learn from Jesus not to focus on behavior modification, church attendance, or religious externals.

Training children to obey can be so consuming that we lose sight of the ultimate goal of discipleship. Jesus got to the heart of the matter. When mentoring his disciples, he focused on important truths of character, motives, and honoring God.

Jesus continually warned his followers not to concentrate on minor issues. He said to the rule-following Pharisees: "Hypocrites! For you are careful to tithe even the tiniest income from your herb gardens, but you ignore the more important aspects of the law—justice, mercy, and faith. You should tithe, yes, but do not neglect the more important things. Blind guides! You strain your water so you won't accidentally swallow a gnat, but you swallow a camel!" (Matthew 23:23-24).

As we answer our children's questions, we would be wise to intentionally look beneath the surface. By this I mean we may neglect kindness and compassion in our quest to teach them cleanliness, a work ethic, or obedience. Of course these things are important, just as is tithing. We need God's guidance to point our children to the truths that God values most. Jesus focused more on heart transformation than behavior modification. We can learn to follow his lead as we invest in the lives of our children.

A few weeks ago my teen daughter approached me in tears. She'd had an online fight with a friend. As I read the string of texts, I noticed she had used a bad word in her dialogue, and the other gal had used a whole arsenal of foul language. I reacted strongly to her use of that word—I couldn't imagine it coming out of my sweet girl's mouth, let alone appearing in black and white. A new torrent of sobs came, and she headed toward the bathroom.

The Holy Spirit reminded me not to strain a gnat and swallow a camel. I don't like bad language and we would address that subject later. For now, I needed to hug my daughter and comfort her. She needed compassion, not chastisement. I should have looked at what was going on in her heart rather than get tripped up by one behavior that I wanted to modify.

What about you? When it comes to engaging your child in spiritual conversations, do you find yourself acting more concerned about outward behavior or internal transformation?

Let's look more specifically at how Jesus sought to help his disciples learn not to strain gnats and swallow camels. After healing many people, feeding four thousand, and teaching the crowds, Jesus asked his disciples some important questions. He started with a general one and then moved into a more personal inquiry:

> When Jesus came to the region of Caesarea Philippi, he asked his disciples, "Who do people say that the Son of Man is?" "Well," they replied, "some say John the Baptist, some say Elijah, and others say Jeremiah or one of the other prophets." Then he asked them, "But who do you say I am?" Simon Peter answered, "You are the Messiah, the Son of the living God." Jesus replied, "You are blessed, Simon son of John, because my Father in heaven has revealed this to you. You did not learn this from any human being. Now I say to you that you are Peter (which means 'rock'), and upon this rock I will build my church, and all the powers of hell will not conquer it." (Matthew 16:13-18)

Here we see Jesus use strategic questions to help his disciples learn. By definition a disciple is a pupil or a learner. Jesus started by asking what others thought about his identity. Then he asked straight out what the disciples believed about him. In the same way, we can take opportunities to ask our children questions such as:

- What are all the kids at school saying about _____?
- What do you think about it?

Whether we ask about a situation we've observed in someone else's family or a current event, we can use questions the way Christ did to get to the heart of the matter.

To mentor our children, we need to spend time with them, but our physical bodies aren't enough. Our phones, e-mails, and televisions can easily distract us from being fully present even when we are with them physically. In order to effectively mentor our children, we must be with them mentally and emotionally. We should stay prepared for spiritual conversations, ready to answer their questions and ask a few deliberate ones of our own.

A Practical Approach: Highs and Lows

One practical way we have tried to keep dialogue open in our family is that at mealtime, no phones or handheld devices are allowed. And we go around the table asking each person to describe the highest and lowest points of their day. In these moments we hear what they are excited about as well as what worries them. Sean and I answer, too, to remind them that we are people who experience ups and downs. After they share we ask follow-up questions and often have some of our deepest conversations. Many times spiritual topics surface as we talk about situations with friends, teachers, or sports.

It was at mealtime one night when one of our third-grade twins mentioned something she might not have brought up otherwise. She said her lowest point was when her male teacher made fun of her in front of other students. She was truly upset. We know that Proverbs says, "The first one to plead his cause seems right, / Until his neighbor comes and examines him" (Proverbs 18:17 NKJV). So Sean asked her if she would like him to speak to the teacher about it. When she said yes, he placed a call the next day.

My wise husband didn't make accusations but started with questions. The teacher said the situation had been bugging him, and he knew he needed to apologize. He hadn't intended to hurt her but had realized by her reaction that he had. He thanked my husband for the call and took the opportunity to apologize to our daughter at school. She came home beaming; she knew that her feelings mattered to both her dad and her teacher.

Whether you describe highs and lows at dinner or take time to chat in the car, in the kitchen, or at bedtime, it's important to keep asking questions and listening patiently.

- What can you do to open up more dialogue with your child? What questions can you begin to ask?
- How can you sharpen your listening skills when your child asks a question or shares his or her heart?
- What efforts can you make to focus more on the real issues rather than externals?

2. Jesus gave his disciples instructions and occasions to go out on their own.

After the disciples had watched Jesus teach and heal, he gave them opportunities to practice the principles they had been taught.

> One day Jesus called together his twelve disciples and gave them power and authority to cast out all demons and to heal all diseases. Then he sent them out to tell everyone about the Kingdom of God and to heal the sick. "Take nothing for your journey," he instructed them. "Don't take a walking stick, a traveler's bag, food, money, or even a change of clothes. Wherever you go, stay in the same house until you leave town. And if a town refuses to welcome you, shake its dust from your feet as you leave to show that you have abandoned those people to their fate." So they began their circuit of the villages, preaching the Good News and healing the sick. (Luke 9:1-6)

While we don't forget age-appropriate boundaries, we know mentoring involves slowly giving children more responsibility as they grow and mature.

We need to teach them how to be independent. The goal of mentoring is to reproduce in others what we have learned ourselves. Doing for our children what they are capable of doing themselves can cripple rather than help them. For example, when they are able to make their own beds, we should ask them to do it. Are you like me? Sometimes as a parent I can be so controlling about how things are done that I'm not willing to hand over responsibility.

Children are often much more capable than we realize. While the way they do things may not meet our high standards, we miss a great step in mentoring when we don't allow them to grow independent by learning to do things for themselves. For example:

- Preschoolers can pick up their own toys.
- Elementary-school students can do basic chores like gather up laundry or take out trash.
- Middle-school students can make their own lunches.
- Teenagers can write their sports schedules and school meetings on a family calendar.

Recently my daughter had washed the dishes, and when I went to put them away the next day, I found them greasy and covered with stuck-on food. She was capable of doing a better job. I knew I should wait and have her rewash the dishes, but honestly, I dreaded the battle of wills, instruction, and her attitude. So I just cleaned them myself. It wasn't a good mentoring moment. I did talk to her about it later, but this proved much less effective than if I had asked her to do it herself.

Jesus taught and healed, but then he sent his disciples out to do it on their own. He risked their attempting difficult things and making mistakes.

- As you think about your children's ages and abilities, is there anything you continue to do for them that they are capable of doing for themselves?
- What responsibility can you turn over to them so that they can learn through experience?

When I ride with someone to a destination, I don't usually pay much attention to where I'm going. But when I'm in the driver's seat, I must navigate the way. The next time I go somewhere, I'm much more likely to know the way if I've driven there myself. One day, our kids will be in the driver's seat of their own lives without us in the car. We can show them how to manage time, accomplish tasks, and relate with people. But we also need to let them practice trying these tasks on their own so they learn through success and failure.

My neighbor told me how her deaf son, who could hear via cochlear implants, never wanted to order at fast food places when he was young because his speech was affected. His mother recalled the day she made him go up to the counter and order his own food. He was scared and unwilling. Although it would have been much easier for her to just do it for him, she encouraged him but firmly told him he would have to do it if he wanted to eat. He was hungry, so he finally faced his fear and placed his order. With time and more practice, he eventually became comfortable interacting with strangers.

Like this mother, we must encourage our children to try things even when they might not feel ready. Sometimes as parents we secretly like their dependence on us. It makes us feel needed. But as we follow Christ's example, we must give our children opportunities to go out on their own, even if it just means letting them order their own food, walking without holding our hands, or cleaning up their rooms without our help.

Sometimes our children may struggle with new responsibilities and need additional help. Other times they will completely fail at a task. The disciples did both. Struggle and failure are part of the learning process.

3. Jesus used the disciples' mistakes and failures as learning opportunities.

In Matthew 17 the disciples found they couldn't cast a demon out of a boy. They tried and failed, so Jesus stepped in. He rebuked the demon and it left the boy: "Afterward the disciples asked Jesus privately, 'Why couldn't we cast out that demon?' 'You don't have enough faith,' Jesus told them. 'I tell you the truth, if you had faith even as small as a mustard seed, you could say to this mountain, "Move from here to there," and it would move. Nothing would be impossible'" (Matthew 17:19-21).

This often-quoted passage of Scripture came on the heels of the disciples' failure. Jesus used their lack of faith as an opportunity to teach them. He didn't shame himself as a teacher for his disciples' weaknesses; instead he utilized failures as teachable moments. In the same way, as our children make mistakes, rather than see their inabilities as an F on our parenting report card, we can help our kids learn to fail forward.

When our children have done something wrong, we can capitalize on that mentoring moment. Even if they lie, cheat, neglect a chore, or refuse to share, we can use their bad behavior to highlight God's character and teach them more about what it means to be a follower of Jesus.

We find another example of Jesus mentoring his motley crew when they argued amongst themselves. Boy, can I relate to quarreling among the ranks! In Matthew 18 we read:

> About that time the disciples came to Jesus and asked, "Who is greatest in the Kingdom of Heaven?" Jesus called a little child to him and put the child among them. Then he said, "I tell you the truth, unless you turn from your sins and become like little children, you will never get into the Kingdom of Heaven. So anyone who becomes as humble as this little child is the greatest in the Kingdom of Heaven." (vv. 1-4)

Even after Jesus had already communicated this message, these same disciples had a similar dispute at the Last Supper: "Then they began to argue among themselves about who would be the greatest among them. Jesus told them, 'In this world the kings and great men lord it over their people, yet they are called "friends of the people." But among you it will be different. Those who are the greatest among you should take the lowest rank, and the leader should be like a servant'" (Luke 22:24-26).

In both instances the disciples were concerned about who among them was the greatest. At the table where Jesus has just offered the first communion, this became the disciples' concern. In fact they were arguing! In both instances where they worried over their positions in God's kingdom, Jesus used relatable illustrations to help them understand spiritual truth.

Jesus taught them that children and servants possess great faith and leadership abilities. Even when the disciples couldn't cast out a demon and spent time bickering, Jesus continued to teach and train in spite of their lack of understanding. In the Garden of Gethsemane, Jesus asked his disciples to pray, and they fell asleep (Luke 22:45-46). How like children they were—and we often are!

Our children can exasperate us when they argue even after we have taught them a better way. Sometimes, to our frustration, they don't follow our instructions. Jesus showed us that a good mentor just keeps training and using failure as an occasion to move forward.

- What is your usual attitude or frame of mind when your child doesn't follow your instruction or example?
- How can you begin to see your child's mistakes as opportunities for him or her to fail forward?
- How does Jesus's response to the disciples' lack of faith and arguing convict and/or inspire you in mentoring your child?

4. Jesus taught his disciples to mentor others.

Jesus not only modeled good mentoring but also trained his disciples to mentor others. In Matthew 28:19-20, Jesus commissioned his disciples to "go and make disciples of all the nations." He gave them specific instructions, saying they were to baptize these new disciples and teach them everything he had taught them. We call this the Great Commission.

We see other examples of leaders teaching mentoring in the Bible, such as Elijah with Elisha and Paul with Timothy. I love what Paul wrote to his young protégé Timothy: "You have heard me teach things that have been confirmed by many reliable witnesses. Now teach these truths to other trustworthy people who will be able to pass them on to others" (2 Timothy 2:2). Paul was teaching Timothy a practical mentoring principle.

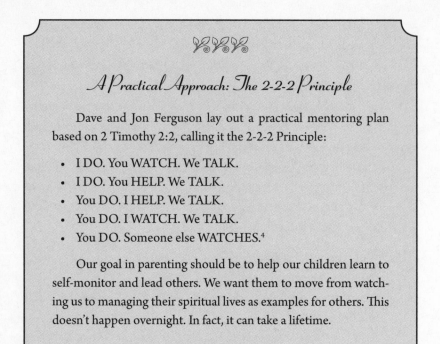

A Practical Approach: The 2-2-2 Principle

Dave and Jon Ferguson lay out a practical mentoring plan based on 2 Timothy 2:2, calling it the 2-2-2 Principle:

- I DO. You WATCH. We TALK.
- I DO. You HELP. We TALK.
- You DO. I HELP. We TALK.
- You DO. I WATCH. We TALK.
- You DO. Someone else WATCHES.[4]

Our goal in parenting should be to help our children learn to self-monitor and lead others. We want them to move from watching us to managing their spiritual lives as examples for others. This doesn't happen overnight. In fact, it can take a lifetime.

As you consider the steps of the 2-2-2 Principle in light of mentoring your child, which aspect comes the most naturally for you? Which one do you struggle with most? I often do a lot of talking but sometimes struggle with helping. Other times I overhelp and need to focus more on just watching and encouraging.

We can learn from the life of Jesus and the example of the apostle Paul to be proactive in mentoring our children spiritually. We won't just stumble upon a close relationship with our children. As parents, we desire to know and love our children well. What do we hope they say to their friends when they're older about how we pursued closeness with them?

When I asked my twelve-year-old daughter what made her feel close to me, her answers were simple but not easy to execute consistently. She mentioned one-on-one dates, unhurried time chatting on the couch, and bedtime prayers.

I polled a number of other parents I know and respect about what drew them near to their parents when they were young and what intentional steps they are taking now to foster closeness in their own children's hearts. The answers led to two practical steps.

1. *Know your child.* How would you describe his or her personality, preferences, and interests? You can spend lots of time talking to your child, but if you don't study your child, you won't reach his or her heart. Jesus modeled this for us in the lives of his disciples. He knew them and got right to deeper issues.

Reading books that help us understand and relate to our children can guide us. Two of my favorites are *The Five Love Languages of Children* by Gary Chapman and *The Way They Learn* by Cynthia Tobias.

Get creative with your approach. One friend said her mom knew she loved to write more than talk. Her mom started a journal that they passed back and forth. Your child may not be a writer, but he or she does have a method of conversing that may go beyond spoken words. Find out the best language method, and then ask God to give you wisdom to speak it.

2. *Spend time.* My daughter mentioned that I am more focused on listening to her when we go out without her siblings. This time must be intentional. It will not happen on its own.

A Practical Approach: Ideas for Mentoring Your Child

Here are some ways to be intentional in mentoring your child:

- Date your child. Put a chart on the fridge listing the date, activity, parent, and child. This keeps you accountable and stops squabbling over whose turn it is with which parent for a date. Gather questions to spark deeper conversations. Buy a small thoughtful gift and stay away from activities that require little interaction, such as movies. Take walks, learn a sport or skill (tennis, pottery), or be girly (paint nails, fix hair).

- Set a goal and accomplish it together. My twins and I trained for eight weeks to run a 5K during which people threw paint at us. God brought this activity to help us all be more active, but also because it made us spend time together three times a week. The running wasn't always easy, but the race created a colorful shared memory in more ways than one!
- Go away for an overnight trip. Getting away from the tasks of home and visiting a new environment can open the doors for deeper conversations.

As you seek to be intentional in knowing your child and spending time together, asking questions can be a great tool. As we see in the Gospels, Jesus asked a lot of questions—a technique that was both effective and fruitful.

Here's a fun way to ask questions when you are with your child.

A Practical Approach: The Question Game

My kids sometimes roll their eyes when we play the question game, but they seem to love the deeper conversation it brings. I sometimes even bring a list of questions and we take turns picking one to ask. Just be ready to answer honestly when they choose a question for you. Here are my top ten questions to ask a child on a date:

- What have you been thinking about lately just before you fall asleep at night?
- If you could have any superpower, what would it be?
- If you could change one thing about our family, what would it be?

- What is a happy memory you have from one of our family trips?
- If you could ask God a question right now, what would it be?
- Who is your closest friend?
- What is the last dream you remember?
- If you needed to talk about something important and I wasn't around, whom would you go to?
- When did you last help someone else?
- What does your name mean?

No matter what your child's age, you can be proactive as a mentor in his or her life. Not only can you use the date questions listed above, you can refer to the mentoring questions on page 58 to use with your children. The very qualities that you would like a mentor to offer in your life you can model in your mentoring relationship with your child. The seeds you plant in the early years will help ensure a close relationship through the highs and lows ahead. Though you will never do it perfectly, with God's help you can build a deep relationship that your child will want to emulate with his or her own children in the future.

Discussion Topics

Group Discussion Questions

- Take turns completing this statement about a person who invested in your life: "My life would have been very different if I had not met _____."

- What are some practical ways the person you named has mentored or invested in your life?

- If you lacked a mentor, complete this statement: "My life would have been very different if I had had a mentor to teach me _____."

- How close was your relationship with your parents? What factors contributed to the depth of your relationship?

- How would you like your connection with your own children to be similar to or different from what you experienced with your parents growing up?

Getting into God's Word

- Read Matthew 15:1-20. How did Jesus use questions with both the Pharisees and the disciples to teach them spiritual truth?

- Read Matthew 23:23-24. What are some modern-day examples of ways that parents strain gnats and swallow camels when discipling their children?

- Read Matthew 16:13-18. Jesus started with a general question and then moved to a more personal one. How can you implement this method practically in teaching your children?

- Read Luke 9:1-6. How are you giving your child opportunities to try things on his or her own?

- Read Matthew 18:1-5 and Luke 22:24-26. How did Jesus turn his disciples' argument into a teachable moment? What is one small change you can make to approach your child's failures as opportunities?

- Which one of these three principles from Jesus's example most resonates with you and why?

  1. Jesus engaged in spiritual conversations with his disciples.

  2. Jesus gave them instructions and occasions to go out on their own.

  3. Jesus used the disciples' mistakes and failures as learning opportunities.

- What is something from God's Word or this chapter that the Holy Spirit has used to convict or inspire you to make a change in your mentoring relationship with your child?

Digging Deeper

- Read 1 Kings 19:19-21 and 2 Kings 2. What do you learn about mentoring from the relationship between Elijah and Elisha?

- Read Acts 16:1-5; 1 Timothy 1:1-2, 8-19; 1 Timothy 3:14-15; and 1 Timothy 4:12-16. As you look at Paul and Timothy's interactions, what practical truth can you apply to pursue a Paul and train a Timothy?

CHAPTER 4

FINDING COMMUNITY IN THE CHURCH

I can remember when I left a doctor's appointment with my daughter who had recently been diagnosed with alopecia, which I mentioned caused her to lose all her hair. I waited until I had checked her in at school before allowing my emotions to pour out. Right in the parking lot I wept.

When I got home, I let my emotions run their course as I curled up in a ball on my bed and had a pity party before the Lord. When my words were spent, God met me with two instructions. First, he wanted me to trust him with my children, understanding he loved them even more than I did. I agreed. Next, I felt God nudge me to invite some encouraging girlfriends over for lunch to share my struggles and pray.

I did just that, and the time I spent with them was like water to my parched soul. It gave me the courage and strength to get through the next few days. They reminded me of God's truth, pointed out ways they saw God working in my daughter's life, and kept me from the overwhelming sense of aloneness that threatened to distort my vision.

When we face struggles—whether in health, relationships, finances, or anything else—our pain can mar our perception. We need one another. God designed us for relationship, with him and with others. Though sin separated us from God, Romans 5 says, "Our friendship with God was restored by the death of his Son.... So now we can rejoice in our wonderful new relationship with God because our Lord Jesus Christ has made us friends of God" (vv. 10-11). We can have a wonderful friendship with God by putting our faith in Christ.

Human companions are vital, too. My best friend is my husband, Sean. We made a commitment twenty years ago to love and lifelong friendship. It hasn't always been easy, but we have celebrated many joys and endured many difficulties together. As a result, we always have each other to lean on, and our relationship has grown deeper, more trusting, and more life-giving. I love that marriage is a picture of Christ and his church: "As the Scriptures say, 'A man leaves his father and mother and is joined to his wife, and the two are united into one.' This is a great mystery, but it is an illustration of the way Christ and the church are one" (Ephesians 5:31).

We are the bride of Christ. He gave his life on the cross so that we could be reconciled and united with God.

We find throughout Scripture that God does not want us to live our Christian lives in isolation. God himself dwells in community. The Father, Son, and Holy Spirit make up a communal Godhead; we find distinct roles and persons within the Trinity. God designed family and church as places we can experience belonging and relationships.

One of the greatest evidences of this comes in the "one another" passages of the Bible. I've selected only eight of the over two hundred verses that include the words *one another*. Look for these two words in each of the following verses:

> I give you a new command: Love one another. Just as I have loved you, you must also love one another. By this all people will know that you are My disciples, if you have love for one another. (John 13:34-35 HCSB)

> Show family affection to one another with brotherly love. Outdo one another in showing honor. (Romans 12:10 HCSB)

Therefore, let us no longer criticize one another. Instead decide never to put a stumbling block or pitfall in your brother's way. (Romans 14:13 HCSB)

For you were called to be free, brothers; only don't use this freedom as an opportunity for the flesh, but serve one another through love. (Galatians 5:13 HCSB)

Carry one another's burdens; in this way you will fulfill the law of Christ. (Galatians 6:2 HCSB)

With all humility and gentleness, with patience, accepting one another in love. (Ephesians 4:2 HCSB)

See to it that no one repays evil for evil to anyone, but always pursue what is good for one another and for all. (1 Thessalonians 5:15 HCSB)

And let us be concerned about one another in order to promote love and good works, not staying away from our worship meetings, as some habitually do, but encouraging each other, and all the more as you see the day drawing near. (Hebrews 10:24-25 HCSB)

Therefore, confess your sins to one another and pray for one another, so that you may be healed. The urgent request of a righteous person is very powerful in its effect. (James 5:16 HCSB)

We cannot "one another" on our own. The church is not a building or an event. The church is us! It is made up of followers of Christ across the planet. Together we are the bride of Christ preparing for the day our groom will return. And while we have fellow believers around the globe, we need to identify with a local body of believers so we can live out the "one another" statements practically.

God says isolation isn't good for us plainly in Hebrews 10:25: "Let us not neglect our meeting together, as some people do, but encourage one another, especially now that the day of his return is drawing near." He's laid out clear prescriptive instructions in his Word about church leadership, discipline, and order and care within the church family. Within that framework, the church in our modern culture can thrive with great variety and creativity.

I know modeling church commitment to our children can be tough if church experiences have wounded us. I've experienced some of my most difficult hurts—and my greatest joys—through Christian relationships. I've met many parents who don't want to go to church or involve their children with one because of past pain. Perhaps that describes you. I understand the reluctance to want to get involved again, but we can't let our hurts prevent us from obeying Christ's command to be involved in the church he instituted. Here's why.

To be a follower of Christ means living real, messy life alongside other believers so we can practice all those "one anothers" for God's glory. Through conflict we learn to forgive. With differences we begin to accept each other. At church we find a place to study God's word, serve, worship, and love alongside fellow sinners.

No church will ever be perfect. Someone once told me to find a church where I was 80 percent happy. He said I'll never be at 100 percent as long as humans lead the church! Humans sin. They forget to call back. They drop balls. They make decisions in ways I wouldn't. Then with the 20 percent I don't like, I can either choose to accept the differences or try to bring change where it's needed.

What do you hope to model for your children concerning the importance of church community?

MODELING

If you want your children to experience authentic community as part of the bride of Christ, they need to see you involved. When we drop them off at kid activities and head home to watch television, we aren't communicating the value of fellowship. While social media, texting, and e-mail with fellow believers can be great means of communicating, they cannot replace real-life interactions.

Churches come in all shapes and sizes. It's not about finding the right kind. Instead, we must find the one where God is calling us to worship him and fellowship with other believers. I know church shopping can be exhausting and daunting. How you go about it will communicate volumes to your children.

Will you go with a consumer attitude, asking if a church will offer you easy parking, quick sermons, programs that wow you, music you love, and services that fit your schedule? We are consumers everywhere else! On products from groceries to swimming lessons, we are on the prowl to get the most bang for our buck. If we find phone service that is cheaper or better, we switch. Most of us are not loyal to brand names or traditional methods. We want the best item at the cheapest price. I'm one of these consumers: give me the warehouse clubs and no frills! But the church is not a product, and its people are not consumers. We should not vacate one pew in search of another for a "better deal."

Since we live in a consumer-based culture, it's natural for this thinking to bleed over into our search for a church family. We must guard against unknowingly communicating to our kids that a church family must primarily be convenient and comfortable for us. Nowhere do we find this attitude toward church in Scripture. We also don't see it in the life or message of Jesus. Let's look at a few principles from his life that we can apply in our quest to model Christian community for our children.

1. Jesus calls us to a life of sacrifice, not convenience.

First Jesus said to his disciples, "Now I say to you that you are Peter (which means 'rock'), and upon this rock I will build my church, and all the powers of hell will not conquer it" (Matthew 16:18). Right after he communicated his intent to build his church, he instructed, "If any of you wants to be my follower, you must give up your own way, take up your cross, and follow me" (Matthew 16:24).

Whether we are already part of a church family or in the process of looking for one, our attitude toward fellow Christians should be one of loving sacrifice. This means not always doing what we want to do, but looking for what's best for others in our church community. We must make church gatherings a priority so we can worship God corporately and encourage others. We can't do the latter when we don't attend!

When our children participate in age-appropriate church programs, our family has struggled with how sports practices and kids' events can take over Sunday mornings or midweek evenings. It's been challenging to navigate commitment to a team as well as to a church body when we want to model putting God first in everything. We certainly want church attendance to be the priority, and we make missing a church activity or service the exception rather than the rule.

Someone once said to us that attendance doesn't equal commitment when it comes to church involvement. I mentally chewed on that statement for a while. My husband and I always tell our church members that we are not the attendance police. We certainly don't want church members to attend out of compulsion, guilt, or fear of appearing uncommitted. We want people to attend church services, events, or small groups because they want to find deep relationships and worship God with others so they can follow God. He designed us to "one another," and we can't do that with other families if we don't show up.

I wonder how a teacher, coach, or employer would feel about the stance that attendance and commitment aren't related? While sometimes family events, vacations, or sports keep us away from gatherings at our church, other times I have to admit I just don't feel like attending the Sunday service or a small-group Bible study. After a busy week, staying in bed or taking a quiet pajama day sounds inviting! I understand the temptation to just skip it, especially when the weather is rainy or cold or both. But I've found that pushing past the desire for what is easy and comfortable to live life the way God calls me to—in community—is well worth it.

Since Sean is a pastor, we don't get too much choice in the skipping department, and honestly I'm glad. Once I'm worshiping God alongside my church family or hearing God speak to me when I study God's Word with friends, I'm always so happy I came!

- How have you seen the rewards of choosing sacrifice over comfort in your church commitment?
- Does your sacrificial attitude reflect the posture you hope your children will take when they are adults?

2. Jesus forgave others even in the face of betrayal and heartache within his faith community.

I've heard it said that there is no pain like church pain. I believe this is because within a local body we are supposed to get close in community: we share meals, study the Bible, talk about our problems. Unfortunately, along the way we often hurt one another. We say offensive things. We leave people out. Sometimes leaders abuse their power within the church.

Jesus knew what it felt like to have someone he loved, taught, and ministered alongside turn on him when it really mattered. Though Judas had been one of the twelve disciples who had watched Jesus heal, teach, and display God's love and kindness, he betrayed Jesus with a kiss. Jesus experienced betrayal at the hands of someone who had once been close.

Have you felt that kind of pain? That's often what keeps us from fully engaging in community again. Yet Jesus calls us not to give up. He said the following knowing that Judas would betray him:

> You have heard the law that says, "Love your neighbor"
> and hate your enemy. But I say, love your enemies! Pray

> for those who persecute you! In that way, you will be
> acting as true children of your Father in heaven. For he
> gives his sunlight to both the evil and the good, and he
> sends rain on the just and the unjust alike. If you love
> only those who love you, what reward is there for that?
> Even corrupt tax collectors do that much. If you are
> kind only to your friends, how are you different from
> anyone else? Even pagans do that. (Matthew 5:43-47)

To be a Christ-follower is to commit to a local church body knowing that you risk getting hurt or even betrayed. You can model for your child that even though close relationships can be challenging, they are worth it. And when someone does hurt you, through the power of Christ you can become a Christlike forgiver and love everyone—even your betrayers. It's not natural; it's supernatural, and it's one of the ways we prove we are disciples of Jesus.

- How have you struggled to forgive someone in your church?
- If you haven't experienced any pain in church relationships, what is the depth of your relationships within the body?
- How would you like to respond, as an example for your children, when others at church offend you?

3. Jesus calls us to function within the body for the benefit of others.

The Bible talks of the church as the body of Christ, with Christ as its head:

> The human body has many parts, but the many parts
> make up one whole body. So it is with the body of
> Christ. Some of us are Jews, some are Gentiles, some
> are slaves, and some are free. But we have all been bap-
> tized into one body by one Spirit, and we all share the
> same Spirit.
>   Yes, the body has many different parts, not just
> one part. If the foot says, "I am not a part of the body

because I am not a hand," that does not make it any less a part of the body. And if the ear says, "I am not part of the body because I am not an eye," would that make it any less a part of the body? If the whole body were an eye, how would you hear? Or if your whole body were an ear, how would you smell anything?

But our bodies have many parts, and God has put each part just where he wants it. How strange a body would be if it had only one part! Yes, there are many parts, but only one body. The eye can never say to the hand, "I don't need you." The head can't say to the feet, "I don't need you."

In fact, some parts of the body that seem weakest and least important are actually the most necessary. And the parts we regard as less honorable are those we clothe with the greatest care. So we carefully protect those parts that should not be seen, while the more honorable parts do not require this special care. So God has put the body together such that extra honor and care are given to those parts that have less dignity. This makes for harmony among the members, so that all the members care for each other. If one part suffers, all the parts suffer with it, and if one part is honored, all the parts are glad.

All of you together are Christ's body, and each of you is a part of it. (1 Corinthians 12:12-27)

Christ is also the head of the church,
   which is his body.
He is the beginning,
   supreme over all who rise from the dead.
   So he is first in everything. (Colossians 1:18)

Christ is the head, but he has called us to function as other parts of his body. This means that he may call us to attend a church service, meeting, or outreach event for someone else's benefit rather than our own. I've heard people say, "I don't need to attend a group. I learn a lot in my own personal study." "My kids don't really like youth group, so I just do devotions with them at home." What we sometimes forget is that we also participate in community for the sake of others.

You might have insights to share in a group Bible study that would be beneficial to someone else. Your teen might be able to encourage another student who needs it desperately. Church is not all about us! Jesus told us to take up our cross. Sometimes it means going when we don't feel like it and focusing on others' needs rather than our own.

Being part of a church family is not just about enjoying a place that has all the qualities on our checklist, makes us feel good inside, and gives us a place to go for special occasions and holidays. It's about commitment to a group of people whether we feel like being around them or not. This means working through conflicts, dealing with people who are different from us, and forgiving when others offend us. It also entails prioritizing church gatherings so that we take the time to build real relationships to encourage and serve others.

If we approach church community seeking to love others, we will find blessings coming our way. We should not attend services expecting to receive from the body. Usually we receive without our seeking it when we fully invest ourselves in the lives of others.

When our daughter Abby first began to lose her hair, our church family showered us with help, prayer, and encouragement. They seemed to anticipate our needs even before we realized them. It was clear many had endured their own trials and so knew just how to help and what to say (or not to say). Through hats, notes of encouragement, and prayers, God's love was fleshed out through the body of Christ—just as he designed. Those expressions were God's grace and source of strength to us in moments of despair. We saw Jesus in our church family.

As we model for our children a commitment to community in the good and bad times, we'll find blessings chasing us. Still, we must continually guard against participating in community solely for our own benefit. So many times I've heard statements like:

- "No one from church came to see me or called me." (Did they know you were sick or struggling?)
- "I don't feel connected. Nobody talks to me." (Do you participate in a smaller group setting? Sometimes in a large group it's difficult to get to know people. Have you made efforts to talk to others, or are you waiting for them to talk to you?)
- "Why don't we have this or that ministry or connection opportunity?" (Are you willing to put in the time and effort to help make the change you want to see in your church?)
- "I don't like the music [preaching, lights, temperature] at church." (Have you lost sight of what matters? Church is about worshiping God and fellowshiping with other believers—for their benefit as well as yours—not personally approving of every aspect.)

Remember that little ears are often listening when conversations regarding church take place. You may think they aren't hearing and internalizing in the back of the car or at the dinner table, but they are. And your attitude toward church will affect theirs.

If you have issues with your church, remember to start at the top! Christ is the head of the body. Spend some time in his presence asking for direction and help. We know through the Epistles that the early church had problems just as we have in our churches today. As Christians were often oppressed in those days, they found strength in numbers; they stuck together and worked out their differences. Is it ever appropriate to leave a church for a new one? Of course. But sometimes people head for a new church without trying to work out their problems with leaders or other congregants. It can be easier to avoid than to confront issues, but Jesus tells us that community is worth it.

A Practical Approach:
When You're Thinking of Leaving Your Church

Are you resisting wholehearted commitment to your church? Do you hear people talk about what they love about their church and consider leaving yours for what sounds like greener grass? In moments when we begin to feel this way, we need to ask ourselves how much we value our relationships within the body. Is our restlessness truly the Holy Spirit leading us to leave, or could one of the following issues be luring us away?

1. We are going through a spiritually dry time. Everyone has them. This is usually not the time to make such a life-altering decision as switching churches. If you can, get past the valley and then evaluate your concerns.

2. We have hurt feelings. Someone within the body has wounded us. Instead of running away from conflict, work toward restoration with the one who offended you.

3. We feel overworked and underappreciated. Seek God's approval, not people's, and establish clear boundaries that protect your family time and personal time. Take a break from a heavy ministry load.

4. Another person has pointed out some church weaknesses we never noticed. Instead of jumping to conclusions or developing a critical spirit, investigate the issue, ask leaders for wisdom and their perspectives, and help develop solutions.

5. Leadership changes occur within the church. Remember the church is a living, growing organism. A new person may not always do things the same way as the leader before. Make sure your irritations aren't personality conflicts. "Different" isn't always bad! Change comes as the church seeks to remain relevant in a changing culture. Worship and follow Jesus, and find the good in every leader.

6. We feel the church isn't meeting all our needs. It isn't supposed to! Jesus is. Have you stopped serving? Have you adopted a Christlike attitude that says, "How can I help out in the church?" instead of "How can the church serve me?"

If you have negative attitudes, irritations, or conflict in your church right now, consider one of these options:

- Meet with a leader to talk more about what is bothering you.
- Volunteer to help in the ministry area where you are dissatisfied in order to be an encourager and solution-oriented aid in making things better.
- Choose not to gossip with others but go straight to the source with questions or constructive criticism.

When considering your church, liken it to your marriage or a favorite friendship. Stay committed through the mountaintops and the valleys. Satan likes us to focus on all the minor differences that lead to discord. He tells us to be self-righteous, condescending, and uncommitted. But the church exists for God's glory, not for personal comfort. Satan wants us to seek self-satisfaction rather than service.

In front of our watching children, we must choose to view the church as God does. It is precious to him, his own bride, and his creation designed with our benefit in mind. May our hearts align with his as we serve and grow through a local body of believers—and may we not postpone this important facet of our discipleship.

Someone told me at a neighborhood party that they have been looking for a church for ten years! Surely in even the smallest town there is at least one gathering of believers who love Jesus and want to follow him by meeting for worship, service, and studying his Word. Finding a local body of Christ-followers in which we can develop authentic relationships and model for our children the importance of church family is critical to our spiritual growth and that of our children.

❧❧❧

A Practical Approach: Finding a Church

If you aren't involved in a church family right now, what should you look for in a church? Consider these important areas of truth and practice when choosing a local body:

- **A statement of faith.** This describes what the church believes about the Bible, Jesus, and foundations of faith such as prayer, missions, and discipleship. (You can usually find a statement of faith on the church website. If not, you can ask for a copy.) Just as families have traditional ways of celebrating special occasions, churches have different ways of expressing the same biblical truths. We can adjust to new traditions just as I had to learn to eat Dutch Apple Flappen every New Year's after I got married. Still, we shouldn't compromise on important theological truths. Find a church where your theology aligns with theirs and choose to compromise in areas of preference or tradition rather than core beliefs.
- **The model of leadership.** Who decides how things run in the church? How the church functions may not seem to matter when you are looking for trendy preaching or cool music. But when real-life issues come up, you will want to know how decisions are made, money is spent, and conflicts are handled.
- **A heart for local and global ministry.** Does the church care about those in their community and beyond who are struggling? Do their budget and programming reflect that the mission to serve others is paramount in following Jesus?
- **A desire to help others have a relationship with God.** Is the church content with the members it has, or is it looking

---

for ways to help others become fully committed followers of Christ? Jesus said he came to heal the sick, not those who thought they were well (Mark 2:17).

Of course we want the preaching to be compelling, but we shouldn't choose a church based on the personality of a pastor whom God may call elsewhere. We want to the music to be pleasant, but our main concern should be worshiping God, not toe-tapping music. Many people choose a church based on where they feel their kids will be happy, but kids can be fickle in their preferences. One day they like something and the next they don't. As a parent, you lead the way in following God's voice to choose a local church family.

In fact, a huge aspect of finding a church should be the personal leading of the Holy Spirit. As we pray, study God's Word, and seek the counsel of godly mentors, the Lord may lead us in ways that don't make sense to us at the time. Though it's best for families to attend the same church, sometimes God may have a different plan in mind.

When I was in high school, my family moved from rural Texas to a suburb of Dallas. We visited many churches, looking for the right fit. My two older siblings were away at college, but my younger sister and I needed a good youth group. My parents had a heart for church planting in low-income communities. We finally settled at an established church that didn't really fit all the criteria.

A few months later the church leaders announced that they were planting another church in a small rural community about twenty minutes away. My parents went immediately, and at first they tried to drag my sister and me with them. Ultimately they realized we needed to stay at the original church to find our own community. They weren't happy that we weren't attending church services together, but God truly led that direction.

In hindsight we see God's wisdom: my sister and I were able to bring teens from the mother church to serve the smaller plant to lead teen meetings and staff their vacation Bible school. It gave the larger youth group an opportunity to serve, and as our parents reminded us of the smaller church's needs, we became catalysts for meeting those needs.

Additionally, God knew that in just a few short years, once my sister and I were in college, he would call my parents to full-time missions overseas. The independence we learned going to church on our own helped us through the next decade with our parents living in Eastern Europe. Also, because my parents attended the church plant, ladies in the bigger church rallied around my sister and me. They invested time in relationships with us. When my parents were gone, we often stayed in the ladies' homes when we visited the town on college breaks.

God is all-wise. He may call you to serve in a church that rubs against your own logic but makes perfect sense in his grand design. For this reason, we must stay in close relationship with him so that we can hear his voice and follow his leading—especially when it comes to finding a church family.

TRAINING

Not only must we model a commitment to church community, we must also be intentional in helping our children find connections within our church family. We want them to grow at every age in a healthy view of Christ's bride. The three insights we found from Jesus about the body of Christ can be at the forefront of our training for our children. Church is:

1. a place we approach sacrificially;
2. a place where real conflicts happen and we have an opportunity to forgive, accept, and serve "one another";
3. a place where Jesus is the head and we are the body functioning for the benefit of others.

As you talk with your children about church, remind them of these truths.

My children have struggled at times when they felt shy entering a new Sunday school class. Other times we fought before church over what they were wearing. Many times I worried too much about what others thought about my children's behavior than my children's attitudes toward Christian community.

If you asked your child, "Why do we go to church?" how do you think he or she would answer? Thinking about that question can help you to teach your child about the importance of relationships within the local church.

A Practical Approach: Encouraging Your Child to Develop Relationships at Church

Just as it's important for you to build relationships within the church, your child needs friendships there as well. Many churches have children's Sunday school classes and/or midweek children's programs where they can learn God's truths in age-appropriate ways alongside peers. This is a great place to start encouraging them in church community.

- Invite families from your child's Sunday school class or midweek ministry over for play dates or dinner at your home.
- Ask the Sunday school teacher or leader of your child's group, "Who do you think would be a good fit as a friend for my child?" Describe your child's personality and interests.
- Greet and initiate conversations with other parents when you drop off your child at his or her class.
- Ask the Holy Spirit to direct you in helping your child find a community of friends through the church.

For the most part we've been blessed: our children have always wanted to attend church services and functions. Friendships they developed were significant reasons. They don't want to miss church activities because they want to see their chums—their community. While they love God and want to worship him, having pals in the church has sure helped.

- What ideas have you implemented to help your child find connection at your church?
- What reasons have your children given for why they don't want to attend church services or functions?

1. Friends

Parents ask me about what to do when their children start to develop friendships with kids who are far from God. I respond that Christ calls us to love everyone, especially those far from him. We don't make them our "projects," seeking their friendship with the goal of changing them in some way, but sometimes we get an opportunity to tell them about our Savior or invite them to a church gathering. We can pray with our children for these friends and love them.

In school and our neighborhoods, our children will rub shoulders with other children who are troubled, live in abusive homes, or face trials we could never imagine. Jesus calls us to befriend those who are hurting. We can be the good Samaritans rather than the religious leaders who step over those who are wounded in our communities.

My one caution is that your child's closest group should consist of those who are like-minded. Proverbs 27:17 says, "As iron sharpens iron, / so a friend sharpens a friend."

When it comes to their inner circle—where our children go for advice and support—we should teach them to be cautious: "The righteous choose their friends carefully, / but the way of the wicked leads them astray" (Proverbs 12:26 NIV). Even within the church we find some people will be:

- Draining. They need love and lots of support, and they might be working through addiction, grief, or crisis. We serve them in Christ's power but might feel worn out after time spent with them.
- Neutral. We don't feel drained but also don't feel especially nourished after being with them.
- Replenishing. They encourage and fill us when we spend time together. Often they feel the same way when leaving our presence.

One person may be all these different things in our children's lives at various times. We must help them learn that their closest circle should offer support and unconditional love. We should also help them realize that they shouldn't always seek relationships for what they can get out of them. At times they must listen to and love those who are draining in order to follow Christ. By equipping our children in spiritual conversations about the balances of friendship, we will help them make good decisions about finding nurturing Christian community.

- What conversations have you had with your child about friendship?
- What stories could you share with your child about your own personal journey with finding godly friends?

2. Multigenerational Relationships

Not only do we want our children to find peers and friends in the local body of Christ but also we should encourage developing multigenerational relationships. When my twins turned thirteen, I asked them to write a list of women from our church who had influenced them. I explained that I was planning an evening where each person would write them a letter about what it meant to be a godly woman. Each lady would tackle a specific topic like prayer, purity, or friendship.

The girls listed eight women who had influenced their lives. Some of them were friends of mine who had interacted with them through family dinners, game nights, or small-group events. Others were young moms to whom my girls had been mothers' helpers when they were younger. A few were women who had been Sunday school teachers or youth leaders. I had expected just two or three women, but they wouldn't budge on cutting anyone from the list!

Helping your child find multigenerational community gets more difficult in a church in which kids are dropped off at classes or groups. When everyone goes in a different direction, we'll need to be more proactive about engaging in family-centered church relationships. Children's ministry and youth groups help our kids connect with peers and attain age-appropriate learning. But community should not begin and end with these programs for our children.

In their book *Sticky Faith*, Drs. Kara E. Powell and Chap Clark identified intergenerational relationships as a key in helping faith "stick" with our kids through the long haul. They write, "Sticky social webs don't happen by accident. You need to build those relationships with regular contact. As with most aspects of parenting, we have to be intentional. Just as a spider meticulously creates its web, so we must devote significant time and energy to surrounding our children with intergenerational relationships."[5]

A Practical Approach: Connecting Multigenerationally

Here are some of the best ways to help kids connect with people of all ages in the church:

- **Invite other families over for dinner.** Many times we are so busy with our own schedules that it's just easier to turn inward. To plan a date, clean the house, and make a meal can be overwhelming. It's so worth it, though! Make it a little easier on yourself by ordering pizza, using paper plates, and not worrying over a perfect house. Make a list of families you want to have over and post it on the fridge. Then set a date with one family at a time, a few weeks in advance, for them to join you for Friday family fun night. Brainstorm with your children which families from your church they would like to spend some more time with. The other family can even help set the night's agenda for eating, playing games, watching a family movie, and so on. If that doesn't work for you, find a way to have another family over after a church service or on a weeknight, and make the necessary sacrifices. You'll appreciate how these nights help both you and your children develop a healthy sense of intergenerational community.

- **Host the families in your small group or Bible study for a cookout.** We've done this every year since our children were small. They love the chaos in the backyard and all the little people running around. It is loud and crazy, and the neighbors joke about our annual gatherings, but my kids smile when they tell stories about water balloon volleyball, relay races, and flashlight tag.

- **Include kids in serving opportunities.** Serving contributes to great community as we sing in nursing homes, host bingo games, sort backpacks at a school-supply drive, or prepare meals at a homeless shelter. Our kids interact with other adults, teens, and children from our church body as we love our community together. (More on serving in the next chapter)

- **Plan events and activities that include all generations.** Church campouts have been an annual favorite, with families spending a weekend helping each other set up tents, cook, and paddle canoes together. I love to watch my kids interact with people of all ages during these weekends. We've also included girls in our women's brunch, had teens serve in our children's Sunday school, and invited the kids to watch the dads on the softball league.

These are just a few of the many ways you can build multigenerational relationships with the people of your church.

- Growing up, did you develop relationships with older role models in your church? Why or why not?
- What is one practical idea you can follow through on to help your child form connections with people from other generations at your church?

The key factor in all of the ideas in this chapter is joining hearts and lives with those in your church. Scripture supports this idea: "So let's not get tired of doing what is good. At just the right time we will reap a harvest of blessing if we don't give up. Therefore, whenever we have the opportunity, we should do good to everyone—especially to those in the family of faith" (Galatians 6:10 NLT 2015). We all get tired, but God calls us to keep doing good—especially to those in the family of faith.

If we want our children to value Christian community, we must give them opportunities to be a part of it. They may not always want to. You might be tempted to skip stuff. We can't do it all. But we can sacrificially spend time loving and serving the people in our church as we work at developing close relationships with other Christ-followers.

As you help your child find community within a local body of believers, you will leave them a legacy of church family. We don't know where our children will go in life or whether we will be present through all of life's challenges. God designed his church members to help one another very tangibly. Modeling and training in the priority of a local church body will help our children learn that they cannot only be God's friends, but they also can have an extended family alongside the other friends of God in their church community.

Discussion Topics

Group Discussion Questions

- Can you think of a time, good or bad, when your church family was a great comfort or support to you?

- What level of commitment do you hope your child will have to a local church body when he or she is an adult?

- What have been the biggest inhibitors to your family's attendance at church services or functions? What changes can you make to prioritize church involvement?

Getting into God's Word

- Read Ephesians 5:25-32. What are some other correlations between the church and marriage? Have you ever felt as if you were "dating" the church rather than being fully committed to it?

- Read the "one another" verses on pages 78–79. Which one of these is the most challenging to live out in the church for you right now? Can you think of any other "one another" verses in the Bible?

- Which one of these three principles from Jesus's example most resonates with you and why?

  1. Jesus calls us to a life of sacrifice, not convenience (Matthew 16:18, 24).

2. Jesus forgave others even in the face of betrayal and heartache within his faith community (Matthew 5:43-47).

3. Jesus calls us to function with the body for the benefit of others (Colossians 1:18; 1 Corinthians 12:12-27).

(If time allows, read each of the corresponding passages and discuss insights you gain about church involvement from the verses.)

- What is something from God's Word that the Holy Spirit used in this chapter to convict or inspire you to make a change in how you model and/or train your child in the importance of church community?

Digging Deeper

- Read Acts 2 aloud as a group. What did the church look like when it began?

- Read Acts 6:1-7. According to verse 1, what began to happen early on? How was the problem handled? What principles can we learn from this example about dealing with discontent in our churches?

- Read Hebrews 13:7-18. What do we learn about our attitudes and instructions toward church leaders? How can we model this attitude of prayer for our leaders?

CHAPTER 5

SERVING OTHERS

For many years our family has attended a Christian summer camp. The college students who work there jump up and down, shouting and singing, as we pull into the main entrance. They valet park our van, unload our luggage, and seem to really enjoy pouring our kids' drinks at meals. They serve like no one I've ever witnessed. And they don't just do this for us, but for every family who attends the camp!

The first year we went, I asked the camp director how he inspired the staff, mostly college kids, to serve with such enthusiasm. They genuinely exhibited joy in helping others. He told me that during training he teaches about Christ's ministry: he washes feet, plays with children, and says the least will be the greatest. He tells these students that they are most like Jesus when they are serving. He also tells them that many of the families coming to camp are overscheduled, tired, and in need of spiritual refreshment. He casts a vision of making a real difference in people's lives by serving them in the great and the small.

I always return home from this week of camp with a greater motivation to rediscover the joy of serving. Albert Schweitzer said, "I don't know what your destiny will be, but one thing I know: the only ones among you who will be really happy are those who will have sought and found how to serve."[6]

We look like Jesus when we serve others. Philippians 2:3-8 says this about service:

> Don't be selfish; don't try to impress others. Be humble, thinking of others as better than yourselves. Don't look out only for your own interests, but take an interest in others, too. You must have the same attitude that Christ Jesus had.

> Though he was God,
>   he did not think of equality with God
>   as something to cling to.
> Instead, he gave up his divine privileges;
>   he took the humble position of a slave
>   and was born as a human being.
> When he appeared in human form,
>   he humbled himself in obedience to God
>   and died a criminal's death on a cross.

Jesus helped others in small practical ways but also in the ultimate act of service: dying a criminal's death on a cross. Did you notice that Paul, the writer of Philippians, said, "You must have the same attitude that Christ Jesus had" (Philippians 2:5)? In a culture obsessed with self, helping our children become fully devoted followers of Christ by taking the posture of a servant can be a daunting task. The narcissism epidemic is real. Authors Jean M. Twenge and W. Keith Campbell write, "The emphasis on self-admiration for children is relatively new. Parents may have always thought their children were special, but until recently they did not expect the rest of the world to treat them that way."[7] Our children are growing up in a culture that screams, "You deserve the best"; "You are superior to everyone else"; "The rest of the world revolves around you"; "Make yourself happy by pouring out resources on yourself."

We see it from the baby bibs with the word *supermodel* embroidered on them to the teens creating personal brands on YouTube channels. The whole concept of selfies and measuring yourself by how many likes you get on social media only aggravates the narcissist tendencies we come by naturally.

Yet for all this emphasis on self, the satisfaction rate doesn't correlate at all. Child anxiety and depression have not been alleviated through a society that promotes self-focus. Instead, it's possible that it has had the opposite effect, particularly among teens.[8] Perhaps the Jesus way of living a life of service and thinking of others as better than ourselves really is the true path to joy, both for us and for our children. We need to promote God-confidence rather than self-esteem. With God-confidence, children see themselves as valuable and important because God created them and has a plan for their lives.

So how do we combat the culture of selfishness surrounding our children? We start just the way we did when looking at the disciplines of prayer, Bible study, mentoring, and church community. We look first at ourselves as parents to see if we are modeling a life of God-confidence and service. By digging into God's Word, we can find applicable principles to encourage and equip us to serve others. Then we take intentional steps to train our children so they can see that real joy comes from following Jesus. And remember, we look most like him when we are serving!

MODELING

When God's love and knowledge are growing in us, we will desire to share them. We were created to serve. Let's look at the life of Jesus to find some principles about service.

1. Jesus taught that loving your neighbor often means getting involved.

One day an expert in Jewish law approached Jesus and asked what he needed to do to inherit eternal life. I love how Jesus used questions to teach and then asked the expert how he understood the answer from the law of Moses: "The man answered, 'You must love the LORD your God with all your

103

heart, all your soul, all your strength, and all your mind.' And, 'Love your neighbor as yourself.' 'Right!' Jesus told him. 'Do this and you will live!' The man wanted to justify his actions, so he asked Jesus, 'And who is my neighbor?'" (Luke 10:27-29).

Scripture includes the explanation that the man was trying to justify his actions. When it comes to serving, we can at times also look for loopholes. Our Savior didn't preach a sermon to this law expert; instead he illustrated how to love neighbors with a story:

> "A Jewish man was traveling from Jerusalem down to Jericho, and he was attacked by bandits. They stripped him of his clothes, beat him up, and left him half dead beside the road.
>
> "By chance a priest came along. But when he saw the man lying there, he crossed to the other side of the road and passed him by. A Temple assistant walked over and looked at him lying there, but he also passed by on the other side.
>
> "Then a despised Samaritan came along, and when he saw the man, he felt compassion for him. Going over to him, the Samaritan soothed his wounds with olive oil and wine and bandaged them. Then he put the man on his own donkey and took him to an inn, where he took care of him. The next day he handed the innkeeper two silver coins, telling him, 'Take care of this man. If his bill runs higher than this, I'll pay you the next time I'm here.'
>
> "Now which of these three would you say was a neighbor to the man who was attacked by bandits?" Jesus asked. The man replied, "The one who showed him mercy." Then Jesus said, "Yes, now go and do the same." (Luke 10:30-37)

The story of the good Samaritan communicates that loving our neighbors means showing mercy by getting involved. We may not see wounded people lying on the side of the road as we drive to the grocery store or take our kids to music lessons, but we can always find people in need of mercy in our communities. So many of our neighbors suffer in ways we might never imagine.

My memory-verse partner leads a local organization that helps families in our community. She told me a few weeks ago about some immigrant fathers deported back to their country. Their wives and children were left behind and received word from their husbands that their country was unsafe and that they should remain in our city. One mother had just given birth. They had no sources of income, struggled to communicate in English, and were genuinely scared. They needed compassionate neighbors. And my friend's organization was meeting that need.

Another family arrived in our city fleeing religious persecution in Pakistan. This pastor, along with his wife and three small children, needed a place to live, food, and Christian support from those of us who live in a place where we are free to serve God. They needed compassionate neighbors to help them while they transitioned to a new life in the United States. Serving them meant sacrificial acts, including providing for basic needs, taking them to run errands, helping with medical care, and showing patience as they struggled to adjust to a new culture.

These stories might sound glamorous, but the sacrifice of time, money, and emotional energy involved on a night when you are fatigued from your own problems lacks luster. Laying aside our own agendas to help others isn't usually convenient or exciting.

In your town I'm sure you will find people who face health crises, job loss, addiction, and other challenges you may never have had to face. God calls us to notice, stop, and offer aid. Sometimes the robbers and bandits in our neighbors' lives come in many different forms. We can't measure others' choices and trials against the backdrop of our experiences. Our journeys have their own set of challenges, but we can't assume others have possessed our same resources or opportunities. Therefore, one thing God doesn't call us to do when serving is judge those we try to help.

The Samaritan didn't stop to interrogate the man on the side of the road to see whether he had taken proper precautions and made wise decisions. He said he would pay the bill even if the stranger's care grew expensive! While we need God's Spirit to direct our helping people so we don't enable or cripple them by keeping them from personal responsibility, we are called to show mercy. Jesus told the religious expert to "go and do the same," referring to the good Samaritan.

- As you think about your life, in what ways can your children see you loving your neighbors?
- Who in your community is in need of physical, financial, or emotional support?
- What serving opportunity have you taken recently that required a sacrifice of time or money?

A Practical Approach: Finding Ways to Serve

If you don't know whom or how to serve, here are some places to start:

- Ask your pastor if he knows of anyone in the church facing a challenging circumstance that you could help with in a tangible way.
- Look for organizations already in place that are serving families in your community. Contact them to see where help is most needed.
- Be present among others who are struggling in your community. It can be scary to go outside of our safe, comfortable neighborhood, especially with our children. While we must be wise and discerning about our safety, we also can trust the Lord to take care of us when he leads.

- Forge real relationships with people from different social and economic backgrounds.

❧❧❧

Loving our neighbor shouldn't be just another task to check off our list of good Christian things to do. Loving neighbors can require authentic, messy, and sometimes difficult relationships.

I have a dear friend who used to be a heroin addict. We met at a park one day and had an instant connection. She has been through recovery and continues on her journey, which often looks different from mine. She grew up facing things I, coming from my safe, loving, though imperfect home, can't even wrap my mind around. We cook together, learn from each other, and face similar parenting issues as both of us are mothers to four kids. I've learned so much from her. She isn't a project; she is my friend. We laugh and cry together. I love her, and I know she loves me. At times she is like a wounded neighbor in need of rescue, and sometimes I am the one desperate for mercy.

To fulfill Christ's command to "go and do likewise," we must look for ways to get involved. Our tendency can be to do as the law expert did: to make excuses or look for ways to justify ourselves. Other times we can be like the priest and the temple assistant crossing to the other side of the road to avoid the world's wounded people. We protest. We have places to go and people to see and kids who need juice! We assume someone else will help them. We are just too busy.

Yet Proverbs 31:8 says, "Speak up for those who cannot speak for themselves; / ensure justice for those being crushed."

- In what ways are you actively modeling for your child loving those in your community who are in need of mercy?
- How have your kids observed you showing compassion to those with less material wealth than your family?

- In what tangible ways can you speak up for those who cannot speak for themselves?

2. Jesus served others even when he was tired and even when he was facing trials.

While we can offer many excuses to explain why we can't fulfill Christ's command to love our neighbor, Jesus dispelled the notion that we shouldn't serve just because we are tired or overwhelmed by our own problems.

Sometimes I feel as though I can't add one more thing to my plate. Laundry, needy kids, helping a friend, work responsibilities, and just getting dinner on the table seem overwhelming. Sometimes in these moments God calls me to rest and neglect other tasks to spend time in his presence and sleep (we'll talk more about rest in the next chapter). Other times God is like a personal trainer in the gym of life, encouraging me to do one more rep with a heavy weight even though I don't think I can. Sometimes we experience short-term pain in serving for the long-term gain of spiritually strong muscles.

Jesus modeled prayer, a knowledge of Scripture, mentoring, and participating in church community so we would have some means of discerning when to serve sacrificially and say no to good things and rest. We find Jesus in Matthew 15 teaching his disciples about inner purity as they struggled to comprehend spiritual truth: "'Don't you understand yet?' Jesus asked" (Matthew 15:16). It can be taxing to help those we are trying to train when they don't seem to get it. On that day, Jesus was having what were probably emotionally draining interactions. Then he traveled north of Galilee to Tyre and Sidon and met a Gentile woman and healed her. After all this teaching, walking, and healing, "Jesus returned to the Sea of Galilee and climbed a hill and sat down" (Matthew 15:29).

After a full day of activity and expending yourself for others, do you just want to sit down and be alone? As an introvert, I have this feeling a lot. After getting kids out the door to school, meeting with women who carry heavy burdens, answering e-mails, sorting through junk mail, and running the kids to their activities, by evening all I want to do is lock myself in my room. Then one of my children says, "Can you help me with my project?" "Will you come pray with me before bed?" "I forgot I need to bring cupcakes to school tomorrow. Can you make them?"

I want to say, "I'm done!" (Okay, sometimes I do say that.) But I hear the Holy Spirit reminding me that he calls me to serve sacrificially; he says I can do one more rep. That's when my spiritual muscles grow stronger. Jesus modeled it well for us. Right after he sat down, "a vast crowd brought to him people who were lame, blind, crippled, those who couldn't speak, and many others. They laid them before Jesus, and he healed them all" (Matthew 15:30).

- When has the Lord called you to continue serving even when you felt exhausted?
- When your strength was gone, in what way did God supernaturally empower you?
- What helps you discern when God is calling you to serve even though you are fatigued, and when he is asking you to rest?

Not only did Jesus serve when he was tired but also he poured out his life during times of trial and grief. In Matthew 14, Jesus heard the news that Herod had beheaded his beloved and faithful cousin, John the Baptist:

> As soon as Jesus heard the news, he left in a boat to a remote area to be alone. But the crowds heard where he was headed and followed on foot from many towns. Jesus saw the huge crowd as he stepped from the boat, and he had compassion on them and healed their sick. That evening the disciples came to him and said, "This is a remote place, and it's already getting late. Send the crowds away so they can go to the villages and buy food for themselves." But Jesus said, "That isn't necessary— you feed them." (Matthew 14:13-16)

Jesus then fed them all with just five loaves and two fish. Even filled with personal loss and pain, Jesus cared for the physical needs of others.

When we're overwhelmed, it seems like a natural reaction to give ourselves time to get through pain or trials, but continuing to serve others can be very therapeutic. Sitting home brooding over loss or just watching television to escape doesn't prove beneficial in working through pain and loss. While we need time to pray, reflect, and allow God to heal our hurts, sometimes he uses serving others as a step in the recovery process.

- Have you ever felt overwhelmed by your own trials but found service to others therapeutic in your own healing?
- In what ways does seeing the needs of others and letting God use you to meet them give you a new perspective?
- What excuses do you need to overcome to model serving others beyond your immediate family?
- Are you willing to serve God even when it's inconvenient?

3. Jesus equated serving others with serving God.

We don't serve worthy people. We serve sinners just like us. Whether it's a weekly commitment or an isolated incident with a stranger, we can bring glory to God when we allow God's Spirit to use us. Jesus painted a picture of how serving on earth echoes into eternity:

> Then the King will say to those on his right, "Come, you who are blessed by my Father, inherit the Kingdom prepared for you from the creation of the world. For I was hungry, and you fed me. I was thirsty, and you gave me a drink. I was a stranger, and you invited me into your home. I was naked, and you gave me clothing. I was sick, and you cared for me. I was in prison, and you visited me."
>
> Then these righteous ones will reply, "Lord, when did we ever see you hungry and feed you? Or thirsty

and give you something to drink? Or a stranger and show you hospitality? Or naked and give you clothing? When did we ever see you sick or in prison and visit you?"

And the King will say, "I tell you the truth, when you did it to one of the least of these my brothers and sisters, you were doing it to me!" (Matthew 25:34-40)

Remembering that serving brings God glory and will be rewarded in heaven gives us the endurance and strength we need to continually pour out our lives in service in a culture that worships selfishness.

For many years I've served as a leader in midweek evening ministries. When my kids were younger, I helped with a children's program that included games, lessons, and Bible memory work. As my own kids transitioned to youth group, I graduated along with them to volunteer in the area where they were involved. Sometimes they complained about my being around, and other times they were glad I was nearby. I didn't let my kids direct where and how I served; I asked the Lord where he wanted me and that always seemed to be near my family.

To be really honest, though, I admit that every time that serving day came around, I usually didn't want to go. I dread evening activities because that is when I'm tired and just want to stay home. Yet I learned early on that my dread isn't related to my desire or joy in serving. It's just my pleasure-seeking nature flaring up. On the ride home I often marvel at how much I loved teaching, talking with students, and seeing God work in the hearts of others. Some nights are definitely more challenging than others, but I feel energized and blessed when I do it.

I will dread it again next week, but I know to dismiss fleeting feelings. First John 3:20 says, "God is greater than our feelings, and he knows everything." He knows I don't feel like leaving my house at night to invest in the lives of the next generation. But he is greater than my emotions. He can help me revise them or even serve others in spite of them.

Don't wait until you feel like serving to serve. You might never want to give up creature comforts like warmth, personal time, rest, home, or hobbies. But the joy you find as you invest your time in others' spiritual lives will far outweigh any sacrifice you make.

- How have you seen glimpses of your service to others yielding benefits that will last into eternity?
- How does knowing that by serving people, you are serving God help you overcome negative feelings or dread about commitments to volunteer?

How do we know where we should serve? Should we just fill the first need we encounter so our kids will learn from our example? That might not be the best idea. Even now my e-mail inbox is filled with requests for me to sign up for things. If I clicked yes to all the requests, I would have a full-time job working in concession stands, calling lines at games, and doing nursery duty at church. We can't do it all.

It's liberating just to say it out loud! Go ahead: *I can't do it all!* We must choose prayerfully, learning to say no to seemingly good things so we can yes to the most important things.

For example, as a parent I have to consider how outside commitments will affect my ability to disciple my own children. We strive for balance. But at times I've made my kids so much of a priority that I've neglected to serve the body of Christ and my community. In other seasons of my life, I've let my family down by accepting too many responsibilities outside of work and home. And when I've taken on too much in either department, I find I don't have margin in my schedule for unexpected needs that arise. If I am overscheduled, I won't have time to take a sick friend a meal or meet a hurting member of our church for conversation. We must guard against extremes of serving too much or too little outside our four walls.

God doesn't leave us alone to navigate the choppy waters of service commitments. As we've seen previously, he gave us his Spirit and his Word. One way he guides us through his Word is through his instruction about spiritual gifts. Many serving opportunities include work that anyone can do: stack chairs, make meals, or love children through presence and time. But we are also wired with spiritual gifts. God has equipped each of us in a special way to serve. Some of us have the spiritual gift of helps, which means God has uniquely equipped us to tangibly help others, but all believers are called to serve.

In the previous chapter, where we talked about the church, we read in 1 Corinthians 12 about the body having many parts that are woven together. Just before the apostle Paul illustrated the church as a body, he taught on spiritual gifts:

> Now, dear brothers and sisters, regarding your question about the special abilities the Spirit gives us. I don't want you to misunderstand this....A spiritual gift is given to each of us so we can help each other. To one person the Spirit gives the ability to give wise advice; to another the same Spirit gives a message of special knowledge. The same Spirit gives great faith to another, and to someone else the one Spirit gives the gift of healing. He gives one person the power to perform miracles, and another the ability to prophesy. He gives someone else the ability to discern whether a message is from the Spirit of God or from another spirit. Still another person is given the ability to speak in unknown languages, while another is given the ability to interpret what is being said. It is the one and only Spirit who distributes all these gifts. He alone decides which gift each person should have. (1 Corinthians 12:1, 7-11)

Notice that every believer receives a gift. You can't claim that God skipped you in the spiritual gifts department! By discovering your gift, you might find service more meaningful as you help others according to the way God designed you. Several other passages give us additional insight into the

113

list of gifts and how they we can use them: read Romans 12:6-8, 1 Peter 4:10-11, and Ephesians 4:11-16 for additional study.

When my twins were two years old, I felt a nudge to leave the older elementary grades where I had taught Sunday school for many years. I figured I should serve in my daughters' class, especially since they were such a handful. After two months I was miserable. I love toddlers in small numbers, but a room full of them crushes me. My daughters hung all over me to the point that I wasn't much use to the rest of the class anyway. Finally someone asked if I would consider returning to the large group teaching time because of a shortage of teachers. I readily left my post in the ankle biters' room to go to a place I felt more equipped.

As I've shared that story with other moms, a few have chuckled that they love toddlers but would struggle to get up in front of a room full of fourth- and fifth-graders to teach the Bible. It's not that one is harder or more important than another. God didn't make us all hands or all feet. He uniquely equips us to serve with a supernatural bent toward some areas more than others.

A Practical Approach: Finding Your Gifts

As you seek to model for your child the importance of serving within the body of Christ and the community, it's important to know your gift. You don't have to figure it out today. It will take study, reflection, prayer, and possibly the input of others who know you well. Here are some steps you can take to discern your God-given gift:

- Study the passages that address spiritual gifts asking God to help you identify any natural strengths or tendencies you know about yourself.
- Take a spiritual gifts class at your church, if one is offered.

- Take a spiritual gifts inventory. There are several online options where you answer a series of questions and then receive feedback on what your gifts might be (www.ministry matters.com/spiritualgifts, www.spiritualgiftstest.com/test/ adult, or www.mintools.com/spiritual-gifts-test.htm).
- Once you have identified some strengths, meet with your mentor or a trusted friend to discuss serving options related to these gifts. Brainstorm ideas and pray together.
- Meet with a staff member or ministry leader at your church to ask where your gifts might intersect with needs at the church.
- Take the next step to serve somewhere related to your gifting. If you discover after a few months it isn't the right fit, try something else. For example, if your gift is:
- Teaching—see if you can apprentice under another teacher whether in kids', teens', or adult ministries.
- Administration—consider helping organize or coordinate events, oversee volunteer scheduling, or assist ministry teams with the organizational aspect of their work.
- Hospitality—join the greeters, coffee team, or welcoming committee.

As you identify and begin using your spiritual gift, you will model the importance of following Jesus by serving. If our children want to know how to obey Jesus, we can show instead of tell them as we serve others just as he did.

TRAINING

In addition to showing our children an example of service, we must also focus our time and attention on helping them learn to participate in it. Once again Jesus paved the way for us.

1. Jesus taught his disciples to follow his example of serving.

In John 13 we find Jesus taking the position of the lowliest slave: he washed his disciples' feet. Since it was an unpleasant job, it was reserved for the least servant. Remember: Roads weren't paved. Animals traveled the same paths as humans, leaving behind their waste. Sandals didn't protect from dust, grime, or animal droppings. Pedicures weren't common practices for these guys. Their feet were dirty and smelly. Can you imagine what the water looked like after washing just one guy, let alone twelve?

Yet Jesus began to wash their feet. Peter protested at first, saying Jesus shouldn't do that for him. Jesus had a way of redirecting Peter. After he explained that those he didn't wash had no part with him, Peter asked the Lord to wash his whole body. I can relate to Peter's extremes! Jesus told Peter that the rest of him was clean; it was only his feet that needed washing. As we serve our family, church, and community, we must guard against an all-or-nothing attitude. Instead we can dig beneath the surface of immediate needs to see the bigger picture of what God wants to accomplish through our acts of service.

Jesus wasn't concerned just with the temporary problem of dirty feet. He wasn't shaming the disciples by initiating because no one else had offered while muttering under his breath—the way I do at times when washing the dinner dishes. Instead he intentionally taught them a valuable lesson about serving:

> After washing their feet, he put on his robe again and sat down and asked, "Do you understand what I was doing? You call me 'Teacher' and 'Lord,' and you are right, because that's what I am. And since I, your Lord and Teacher, have washed your feet, you ought to wash each other's feet. I have given you an example to follow. Do as I have done to you. I tell you the truth, slaves are not greater than their master. Nor is the messenger more important than the one who sends the message. Now that you know these things, God will bless you for doing them." (John 13:12-17)

Jesus didn't wash in silence. He took the opportunity to train his disciples. We see him:

- ask a question: "Do you understand what I was doing?"
- issue a command: "Do as I have done to you."
- give the benefit: "God will bless you for doing them."

A Practical Approach:
Having Spiritual Conversations While Serving

As we serve, we can also train our children through spiritual conversations. We can:

Ask questions: "Do you know why Mom and Dad teach a class at church?" or "Why do you think we volunteer at the shelter?"

I know I'm often rushed when trying to deliver a meal for someone or prepare a lesson for a class I teach. A few times my kids have bemoaned the fact that the meal I'm making isn't for them to enjoy. In those moments I can ask questions and explain how someone just had a baby or a surgery and why they need help. Usually, the kids quickly change their tune and feel compassion for others going through difficult times.

Issue commands: "Clear the dishes." "Put the toys away."

Sometimes we directly state that our children need to serve. Many times the response is, "But this mess isn't all mine." I remind them that I do everyone's laundry, not just mine. I don't just cook dinner for myself. They can't help their selfish tendencies, but we can help them learn the joys of serving by instructing them to do it whether they want to or not.

Give benefits: "After the work is done we can go out for ice

> cream." "Look at how much they appreciated your help stacking the chairs." "You really honored God by your helpful actions."
>
> By reminding our children that hard work yields good results, we help them discover the benefits of service. This is a great opportunity to teach the principle of sowing and reaping: "You will always harvest what you plant" (Galatians 6:7).

2. Jesus taught his disciples that serving others brings blessings.

As Jesus taught his disciples to serve, he reminded them that God would bless them for serving. Our children also need reminders that benefits come to those who serve. The feeling of a job well done, the joy on the faces of those we've helped, and the thought that God is smiling can all be great motivators for repeat behavior.

Not only should we train our kids by dialoguing about our service but also we must provide some hands-on opportunities for them to experience the blessings of serving. When they are young, this can be challenging, but it is possible.

We can start by encouraging them to look for simple ways to serve, such as

- helping out around the house
- doing one of their sibling's chores for them,
- helping prepare and deliver a meal to a new mom
- baking cookies to brighten the teacher's day
- helping a friend pick up the box of markers that they just dropped at school

As we teach children to serve those they know and love, we can make the transition to serving strangers. Cultivating a servant's heart is a process. We start first with our family and friends and then step beyond the walls of our comfort zones.

We've taken our kids into some places that weren't comfortable but where we found neighbors in need of mercy. Several times we did a backyard Bible club in a tough neighborhood. We drove twenty minutes each evening, served a meal, and allowed our children to pair up with adults and teens to go knock on doors each night to bring out the neighborhood kids. When I look back on the pictures of my children acting out the stories of the Bible and playing games alongside kids from these neighborhoods, I know it was right to push past my fears and reach out to love our neighbors outside the bubble of our suburb. And how it has blessed every member of our family!

A Practical Approach: Family-Friendly Serving Ideas

As you think about how you can involve your children with hands-on serving opportunities, do your homework. Talk to parents with older children to get ideas of how they involved their children in serving. Some options to consider when contemplating a family-friendly serving outing:

Adopting a neighbor to help. Identify someone who could really use help with yard work or would enjoy occasional visits or treats. Perhaps a single mom or elderly couple would appreciate a helping hand.

Visiting a nursing home or retirement community regularly. Our small group found a place to sing, play bingo, and really get to know the residents. I admit my kids struggled at first. We chose a low-income resident facility where the conditions weren't always the best. In addition we visited some patients who drooled, were missing appendages, or struggled with communication. At first it was a bit of a shock to their systems, but the ensuing discussions helped them grow and realize many people suffer while the kids feel entitled to ice cream.

My twins developed a special relationship with a sweet older woman with the joy of Jesus in her voice. She had only half of her hair and teeth left from whatever ailments she battled. In addition she had lost a leg in her battle with diabetes. My girls made her cards, prayed for her, and looked forward to visiting her. Until she passed away, I believe the girls brought her joy, and I know she gave something to them—an opportunity to be a blessing.

One of my children's teachers called a nursing home and asked to be connected with a patient with no family in town. They introduced her to a man who was one hundred years old and had no children. His parents and wife had passed away, and he was truly alone. She had her classroom adopt him, assigning them times to visit and bring cards. This teacher gave her students and their families an opportunity to be a blessing and share the joy of serving!

Serving a meal at a shelter. We served with a group of families from our church by signing up for a meal. Different families provided elements of the meal, and we cooked and served it with our children. We sat down and ate with the families in the shelter. One mom planned games for the kids living in the shelter, and ours participated alongside them. My son performed magic tricks for the children. Together we helped feed families who truly needed a meal and to know that someone cared.

Collecting for a food pantry. Most communities have food pantries where families can get basic necessities. My sister asked the organization what items were most needed, then typed up the list. Her children helped her staple the lists to bags with a note for her neighbors letting them know about the needs. The children went with her door to door, alerting people about the bags and the date they would pick them up from everyone's porch. Not only did this help the food pantry but also it brought the neighbors together. So many people thanked her for giving them the opportunity and letting them know of the needs.

Folding, sorting, and cleaning for nonprofit organizations

that serve your community. Most groups that provide clothing and food or serve meals need help with simple tasks. Inquire and volunteer your family to sort clothes or cans. Younger children can fold and wipe things. With your supervision, they can provide a needed service.

Performing simple household tasks for families in need. One year our church leadership asked our church family for names of people who might appreciate having some basic work done for them. They asked for the names of widows, elderly, or people struggling with health issues. An organizer contacted the families to see how we could help and assigned families based on the size of the task. Everything from hauling junk, raking leaves, washing floors and bathrooms, and building a ramp to make a house handicap-accessible happened on that day. My kids saw places that made them grateful for our health and ability to care for our home.

Taking part in prayer walks and canvassing neighborhoods. When we planted a church, we needed to let people know about it, so we divided up neighborhoods and went out putting info on door handles. We stopped and prayed for neighborhoods, chatted with people we met, and helped our kids feel a part of the ministry even when they claimed their feet would fall off!

Taking part in church opportunities. Include your children in service at church. Teach them how you set up the hospitality table. Have them greet at the door with you. Make them your Sunday school apprentices. Ask them to stack chairs and carry things. Show them that service is the norm, not the exception.

Going on mission trips. Traveling with your child to help others can be life-changing. Whether you stay stateside or fly across the globe, serving together can show your child what your words or stories could never convey. The sights, sounds, and smells will help them see that people exist and struggle in many places. My husband has taken three of our four children to Guatemala on individual trips to build, play, and develop relationships in a poor Mayan village. Each of my children has each returned with gratitude for what he or she has and perspective about living in a narcissistic environment.

This is by no means an exhaustive list. It's a starting point. If you have never done any service activity with your children, don't be discouraged. And don't think service has to take over your life. Set a goal of how many times a year you'd like to find a way to serve together as a family. Make it realistic. We aimed for around four times a year and often did it only twice. Still, if we did it twice a year rather than not doing it at all, that's progress!

One helpful thing to remember in training your child about service is to have a debriefing meeting shortly after a serving opportunity. This allows your child to process what he or she has seen and experienced, reflect on the blessings for those serving and being served, and ask any questions that might come to the surface. Use the following worksheet as a guide as you talk about what it means to follow Jesus through service.

Our Family Service Debriefing Worksheet

1. What did you enjoy about this serving opportunity?

2. What didn't you like about it?

3. Did you ever feel uncomfortable? (If so, what made you feel that way?)

4. Before we served, what were your feelings about the project? (What was your reaction inside when I told you what we were going to do?)

5. How did you feel after?

6. How do you think God feels about what we just did? Why?

7. How did others benefit from what we did?

8. Is there anything else you'd like to try now that we've served in this way?

9. Would you want to do this again? Regularly?

10. Read John 13:1-17 together as a family. How do you think we obeyed Jesus's command to serve today? What blessings (good things) did you receive from God by participating in this activity?

By modeling and training our children in service, we can show them the joy of being a Christ-follower. They can see the difference between what they experience after spending hours on social media and hours spent serving. While they may not always have a great attitude, they will look back on these moments with gratitude. Serving others does bring more joy than focusing on self.

Allowing your child to experience that firsthand is a great gift.

- Which one of these ideas perked your interest as one that might work for your family?
- How have you already helped your child learn the joy of serving?
- What measurable goal would you like to set for your family in how regularly you will serve your church and community this year?

As you model service and train your children to look not only to their own interests but also to the interests of others, you will show them what it means to love their neighbor. Sometimes Christians choose to serve in order to make a difference in the world. After serving with the overflow of Christ's love in our own lives, we find out that we end up the ones being blessed by those we serve. Not only will our children experience the joy of serving as we set an example and provide hands-on training for them, they will be equipped to see the needs around them rather than buying into the message of their self-centered culture. If they want to know what Jesus looks like, they will see him through service.

Discussion Topics

Group Discussion Questions

- What is one of the most meaningful service opportunities you have participated in?

- What excuses have you made for why you can't serve outside your family?

- If you could teach your child one thing about serving others, what would it be?

- What fears do you need to overcome in order to love your neighbors who live in scary or dangerous parts of town?

Getting into God's Word

- Read Philippians 2:3-8 on page 102. How is the statement, "You are most like Jesus when you are serving," reflected in this passage?

- Read 1 Corinthians 12:1-11. Share with the group what spiritual gift God has given you. How are you using your gift to build up the body of Christ? If you aren't using your gift, share with the group some ideas you have to begin putting your gift to work.

- Which one of these three principles from Jesus's example most resonates with you and why?

1. Jesus taught that loving your neighbor often means getting involved (Luke 10:27-37).

2. Jesus served others even when he was tired, and even when he was facing trials (Matthew 15:1-30; Matthew 14:13-16).

3. Jesus equated serving others with serving God (Matthew 25:34-40).

(If time allows, read each of the corresponding passages and discuss insights you gain about serving sacrificially from the verses.)

- Read John 13:1-17. How does the example of Jesus inspire you to serve and to teach your child to serve?

- What is something from God's Word that the Holy Spirit used to convict or inspire you to change how you model and/or train your child in the importance of sacrificial service?

Digging Deeper

- Read Mark 10:35-45. How did Jesus help the disciples get over their narcissistic tendencies?

- Read Romans 12:6-8; 1 Peter 4:10-11; 1 Corinthians 12:4-11; Ephesians 4:11-16. What do you learn from these passages about spiritual gifts, and how we can discover and implement them in our lives?

CHAPTER 6

TAKING TIME TO REST

When my twins were babies we had two contraptions that hung from doorposts—some are called Johnny Jump Ups—that they could sit or jump in. They loved to bounce and giggle. It was a great way for them to play while I got dinner made, dishes done, or the endless pile of laundry folded. Once when I realized the squeaking had diminished I peeked around the corner from the kitchen into the hall. Abby's sweet little head rested against the side of her jumper; she had bounced herself right to sleep. Sara kept right on jumping with her twin snoozing in the jumper next to hers.

Even though three of my four kids are now taller than I am, I still like to watch them sleep. They look so peaceful (and they don't talk or roll their eyes). They require much less slumber than they did when they were little, but they still need rest. We all do. God designed our bodies that way. Although God created us in his image, this is one area in which he is different.

If our children ask us if God ever sleeps, the answer is no. While we reflect him in many ways, we cannot forget that he is holy—set apart. He doesn't have the limitations of our humanity. The psalmist wrote,

> I look up to the mountains—
>   does my help come from there?

> My help comes from the LORD,
>> who made heaven and earth!
> He will not let you stumble;
>> the one who watches over you will not slumber.
> Indeed, he who watches over Israel
>> never slumbers or sleeps. (Psalm 121:1-4)

We don't have to wonder if God might be sleeping when we pray. He is fully aware of all that is going on. One of the names used for God in the Old Testament is *El Roi*, "the God who sees" (Genesis 16:13). He doesn't miss a thing. He sees you and me with our crazy busy schedules. In his mercy, he created us with the need for rest. Although he doesn't need it, he modeled it for us because of our tendency to get weary.

Throughout the pages of Scripture, we see an emphasis on the need for rest. In the very beginning, God spoke the world into creation but then intentionally stopped working. He separated light from darkness; put the sun, moon, and stars in place; and created birds and fish, in addition to all plants and animals. Then he made man and woman and gave them dominion over all he had made: "On the seventh day God had finished his work of creation, so he rested from all his work. And God blessed the seventh day and declared it holy, because it was the day when he rested from all his work of creation" (Genesis 2:2-3).

He didn't rest because all that creative energy had left him tired. God never gets worn out.

> Have you never heard?
>> Have you never understood?
> The LORD is the everlasting God,
>> the Creator of all the earth.
> He never grows weak or weary.
>> No one can measure the depths of his understand-
>> ing. (Isaiah 40:28)

No, God rested so we would! We do get weak and weary. God knows our tendency, when driving through life, to ignore red lights and stop signs. We just keep going as if we are Energizer bunnies rather than humans who need time to recharge!

Not only did God emphasize rest in the creation days but also the Ten Commandments include the concept of stopping in the midst of our busyness. God issued a command for the Jewish people through Moses to help them remember:

> Remember to observe the Sabbath day by keeping it holy. You have six days each week for your ordinary work, but the seventh day is a Sabbath day of rest dedicated to the LORD your God. On that day no one in your household may do any work. This includes you, your sons and daughters, your male and female servants, your livestock, and any foreigners living among you. For in six days the LORD made the heavens, the earth, the sea, and everything in them; but on the seventh day he rested. That is why the LORD blessed the Sabbath day and set it apart as holy. (Exodus 20:8-11)

Not only did God encourage rest by modeling it and making it the fourth commandment but also we find him speaking through the prophet Isaiah about the blessings that come for those who choose to rest regularly.

> Keep the Sabbath day holy.
>   Don't pursue your own interests on that day,
> but enjoy the Sabbath
>   and speak of it with delight as the LORD's holy day.
> Honor the Sabbath in everything you do on that day,
>   and don't follow your own desires or talk idly.
> Then the LORD will be your delight.
>   I will give you great honor
> and satisfy you with the inheritance I promised to
>   your ancestor Jacob.
>   I, the Lord, have spoken! (Isaiah 58:13-14)

We can see God promised great benefits to the people of Israel for obedience to his guideline for rest, but how does that translate into our lives as Christ-followers? We aren't under the law anymore. Jesus fulfilled the law. While we know that we have a new covenant under Christ, our God never changes. "I am the LORD, and I do not change" (Malachi 3:6a).

While we don't strictly follow all the practices of the Old Testament law, the concept of rest doesn't fall into the same category as "Don't eat pork." Its necessity is apparent throughout Scripture. As I reflect on Western Christianity and the principles of God's Word, I believe rest is one place where we sorely miss the mark. We constantly fill our schedules without realizing the effect on our children's lives, as well as on our own souls. We need rest—God made it clear. Yet we have a tendency to leave little room for margin.

- How could you explain to your child that God doesn't need rest but that he modeled it for *us*?
- From the Scripture we read, how does God's command for rest challenge your personal and family priorities? What ideas do you have to intentionally plan for rest?
- On a scale of 1 to 10 (with 10 being insanely busy), how overscheduled is your family?

In grade school I used notebook paper that had a thin red vertical line down the page. It was the line where you started writing your spelling words or paragraphs for writing assignments. To the left of that line was the margin. This was the white space where the teacher could make comments or you could make edits to your writing.

In his excellent book on simple living titled *Margin: Restoring Emotional, Physical, Financial, and Time Reserves to Overloaded Lives*, Richard Swenson defines margin and the lack of it:

> Marginless is being thirty minutes late to the doctor's
> office because you were twenty minutes late getting out
> of the bank because you were ten minutes late dropping

the kids off at school because the car ran out of gas two blocks from the gas station—and you forgot your wallet.

Margin, on the other hand, is having breath left at the top of the staircase, money left at the end of the month, and sanity left at the end of adolescence.[9]

Rest becomes elusive when we fill our lives so full of activity that we take things right to the edge of the page. An overscheduled life leaves no room for emergencies, errors, or problems. How many of us enjoy lives without sudden difficulties? They are facts of life. Kids get sick, cars won't start, weather and schedules change. If we're living without margin, the smallest divergence can throw off our plans and cause us to feel completely overwhelmed. Ever had thoughts like this: "Since they changed soccer practice it conflicts with Susie's dance—and that is my day to drive to carpool"? Or "Oh no! That car repair just ate up my grocery money! Now what?"

Without margin in our schedules and finances, it doesn't take much to put us in a state of emergency. I have found myself in a panic when I have taken on too many ministry responsibilities, signed up my children for too many activities, or failed to set boundaries in relationships with needy people. Before I know it my calendar is filled, and I have little room to breathe between the things I *must* do.

Another downfall of lacking margin is the lost opportunity for spontaneity. If a neighbor needs help, someone is giving away free tickets to a special event, or the kids want us to throw a ball in the back yard, we can't take the time because our calendar demands we keep rushing so we don't let someone down.

When we've built margin into our lives, we reap many benefits. We get to have an over-the-fence conversation with a neighbor, which leads to an opportunity to share what Jesus is doing in our lives. When the kids want to have a pillow fight, we can let our guard down knowing these days of play with them are numbered.

Above all else, margin helps us learn to rest. As we've seen, rest is a concept near God's heart. He wants us to embrace relaxation and regularly engage in it. In Isaiah 30:15 God reprimands the people of Israel for failing to do this:

> This is what the Sovereign LORD,
> the Holy One of Israel, says:
> "Only in returning to me
> and resting in me will you be saved.
> In quietness and confidence is your strength.
> But you would have none of it."

He doesn't want us to spend all our time hurrying, filling every empty space on the calendar with activity. He says we'll find strength in quietness. Where does that quietness fit in between everyday tasks such as running errands, going to doctor's appointments, meal planning, and kids' team practices and the other things we add to our schedules such as community involvement, committee meetings, church activities, and ministry or service opportunities? In order to experience rest, we need to evaluate the frenetic pace of our lives.

- Why are we filling our calendars?
- Are we asking the Holy Spirit to guide us about what we choose to commit to with our time?
- What could we cut out to have more time for personal reflection, creativity, and some unhurried family dinners?

I'm tempted by all the good things there are to do. I struggle to start at the red line and leave margin for the unexpected things God wants me to encounter along the way. This year as forms come home from school, volunteer sign-ups are passed around, and people ask for our time, we need Holy Spirit help to know when to say no in order to say yes to margin and God's rest in our lives.

MODELING

Just as we've looked at the life of Jesus to see how he handled prayer, Scripture, mentoring, community, and service, we must also look for his example in the area of rest. He will give us fresh perspective on the Old Testament Sabbath and point us to God's heart.

1. Jesus was never in a hurry.

We don't find these words in the pages of the Gospels: "Then Jesus rushed to get there"; "Jesus hurried to go heal the child"; "Jesus panicked over the food emergency." As a parent, I can sure put my name in sentences with words like *rush, hurry,* and *panic.* How about you?

Jesus served like crazy. We look like him when we serve. Yet he found balance in taking intentional time for rest and downtime between serving opportunities.

1. He began his ministry with forty days in the wilderness praying and seeking the Father (Mark 1:9-13).
2. Several times Jesus left everyone to spend time in prayer and rest (Mark 1:45; 3:13; 6:45-46).
3. Jesus made time for kids. He wasn't too hurried to engage with children (Mark 10:13-14).

The pattern of Jesus's life didn't include frenzied activity to accomplish everything on his to-do list. Nor did he aimlessly wander in his ministry. He followed the leading of his Father in unhurried, purposeful living. The effect of his investment in twelve disciples, coupled with his teaching and healing ministry, led to his death on the cross. Knowing he had only three years of ministry, he still didn't feel pressured to hurry to make sure he accomplished everything. It's true, though, that sometimes he healed, taught, and served even when he was tired. Other times, he set time aside for retreat, rest, and valuing children. Often Jesus went into nature for a break. He visited a wilderness, mountainside, or another quiet place.

His example convicts me in so many ways. When my kids were younger, I was always in a hurry to get out the door and rushed my toddlers through putting on their shoes. I think of times when they lingered if they saw a puppy or a flower, and I encouraged them to walk faster. To this day, all four of my kids are speedy walkers; they learned from Mom, who was always in a hurry to get from one place to another! But rather than live with regret, I'm challenged to make changes going forward. How about you?

I pray as you read this book you don't want to throw it against a wall as so much "pie in the sky" conceptualizing! I know when I read about making changes that seem impossible or goals that seem unreachable, I sometimes want to just throw in the parenting towel. It can be discouraging to hear about things we could or should do in parenting.

But building rest into our schedules is doable and so worth it. When I realized the power of margin, I made some changes. At the top of my list was slowing down and resting more. Instead of allowing guilt to motivate me to overcommit, I looked at Jesus's relaxed example and asked him to help me choose between the necessary and unnecessary. I hope you will do the same. It's never too late to make modifications in the ways we model prayer, time in God's Word, mentoring, church commitment, service, and rest for our children—no matter how many mistakes we've made in the past. Remind yourself, "A relaxed attitude lengthens life" (Proverbs 14:30a TLB).

- How does Jesus's example challenge your pace of life?
- Are you modeling for your children the way you hope they'll deal with schedules, hurry, and rest?
- What's one small change you can make today to live at a more relaxed pace?

2. Jesus showed us how rest moves us from activity to relationship.

The story of Mary and Martha provides a great example where Jesus taught about choosing something greater than worrying.

> As Jesus and the disciples continued on their way to Jerusalem, they came to a certain village where a woman named Martha welcomed him into her home.

> Her sister, Mary, sat at the Lord's feet, listening to what
> he taught. But Martha was distracted by the big dinner
> she was preparing. She came to Jesus and said, "Lord,
> doesn't it seem unfair to you that my sister just sits here
> while I do all the work? Tell her to come and help me."
> But the Lord said to her, "My dear Martha, you are wor-
> ried and upset over all these details! There is only one
> thing worth being concerned about. Mary has discov-
> ered it, and it will not be taken away from her." (Luke
> 10:38-42)

Notice Martha's attitude. She was preparing a big dinner, complaining about her sister's lack of help, and worried and upset over household cares. We've all been there; none of us can judge her! We have so much to accomplish, especially when people are coming over for dinner. When others around us rest in the midst of all that needs to be done, we cry foul. When I decide that the house needs to be cleaned immediately and observe my husband relaxing, I ask Martha's question—only less politely: "Jesus, why isn't he helping me?" When we are focused on tasks, we can miss out on relationships.

There is a time to roll up our sleeves and tackle the work: "For everything there is a season, / a time for every activity under heaven" (Ecclesiastes 3:1). God showed us through the creation account that he established a time for work and a time for rest. King Solomon talked about the need for rest and leisure in Ecclesiastes 3:

> What do people really get for all their hard work? I have
> seen the burden God has placed on us all. Yet God has
> made everything beautiful for its own time. He has
> planted eternity in the human heart, but even so, people
> cannot see the whole scope of God's work from begin-
> ning to end. So I concluded there is nothing better than
> to be happy and enjoy ourselves as long as we can. And
> people should eat and drink and enjoy the fruits of their
> labor, for these are gifts from God. (Ecclesiastes 3:9-13)

Martha served, but she did it while frustrated and complaining. She missed out on something greater as Mary sat at Jesus's feet and listened. Mary's choices included slowing down, resting, and being with Jesus.

God knows our tendency toward workaholism. Rest forces us to lay down our desire for self-sufficiency and endless list of tasks. Admitting that we need rest can be humbling. I want to do it all, and I don't want to admit that I can't! God's call to stop our work reminds us of our dependence on him. But the truth is, we can work ourselves to death because the to-do list will never all be completed. The laundry keeps coming. When one work project is finished, another one appears. Let's not even talk about the overflowing closets and junk drawers!

We need discernment, through the Holy Spirit's power, to know when to put our unfinished work aside and choose something better—like rest or play. When my kids were small they would beg me to play dolls or hide and seek with them. While we need to model our work ethic and help them learn that we aren't at their beck and call, I'm glad for the times I stopped to enter their worlds and play. They are watching us attempt to balance work and leisure.

- In what ways can you find Martha-thinking creeping into your attitude toward all you have to accomplish? (Would your children describe you the way we describe Martha—that is, distracted, worried, task-driven?)
- How can you prioritize relationships over activity in your daily routine?

3. Jesus taught us God's heart behind the Sabbath.

Jesus and his disciples were walking through grain fields one Sabbath and broke off grain to eat. The Pharisees criticized them for "working" on the Sabbath. This is another example of the Pharisees straining a gnat and swallowing a camel. They focused on letter of the law instead of God's heart behind his commands. By dwelling on minutia, they missed the bigger picture.

Jesus responded by reminding them how King David ate sacred loaves of priestly bread when he and his men needed food. "The Sabbath was made to meet the needs of people, and not people to meet the requirements of the Sabbath. So the Son of Man is Lord, even over the Sabbath!" (Mark 2:27-28).

Jesus taught that rest is *for* us. We don't need rest just to rejuvenate so we can work more. Rest has value in and of itself, but we shouldn't get so caught up on the rules of rest that we miss its purpose. Jesus is Lord over the Sabbath. He is our source of rest.

In Hebrews 3, we find Jesus described as greater than Moses. The writer speaks of the people who wandered in the wilderness: "So we see that because of their unbelief they were not able to enter his rest" (Hebrews 3:19). Then Hebrews 4 tells us that Jesus himself is our rest—the fulfillment of the Sabbath that God ordained.

Many rituals of the Old Testament foreshadowed the Messiah. They were glimpses of what would happen when God sent his own Son to earth. The sacrificial system is a great example. We no longer offer animal sacrifices because Christ was the final payment for sin. In a similar way, Jesus fulfills the law of Sabbath as our final rest. We no longer live under the Old Testament laws because they existed to show us our need for a Savior. In Galatians we read, "The law was our guardian until Christ came; it protected us until we could be made right with God through faith" (3:24).

From the fuller revelation of the New Testament, we find that we are no longer bound to strict Sabbath observance; however, just because we no longer live by Old Testament law does not mean God wants us to become workaholics! It means we have freedom rather than law to govern our rest.

That freedom is not an excuse to neglect rest. Jesus longs for us to come to him in our tired states. We find his words of invitation in Matthew 11:28-30: "Come to me, all of you who are weary and carry heavy burdens, and I will give you rest. Take my yoke upon you. Let me teach you, because I am humble and gentle at heart, and you will find rest for your souls. For my yoke is easy to bear, and the burden I give you is light."

Jesus wants us to find rest for our souls. Before we can teach this concept to our children, we must first model it in our own lives.

We need to be careful about two extremes as we enter God's rest with a New Testament mentality.

1. We must guard against overspiritualizing our times of rest. Jesus wasn't a kill-joy who thought we should do nothing beyond eating, working, sleeping, and praying. Leisure has value! He walked, talked, probably played with children, and lounged over meals. All that we define as rest doesn't need a "Christian" label. We aren't limited to reading the Bible, watching Christian movies, or listening to worship music to experience God's kind of rest. A walk in a nature preserve or curling up with a good novel might be the way you unwind.

2. Acting selfishly can be another extreme in approaching Sabbath rest. Rest isn't an excuse for more "me time." We can't hide behind God's desire for rest as an opportunity to do whatever we want. If we aren't careful, our rest can become sinful, and that's not the example we want our children to follow.

Instead, the goal is to find habits and activities that are truly restorative to our souls. These might vary from person to person. Often things we default to in our downtime aren't things that leave us feeling rested afterward. Marathon hours in front of the television or gaming system can sound good, but how many of us truly feel reenergized as we walk away from them? Scrolling through social media usually leaves me overloaded with information about everything from someone's pet's surgery to an acquaintance's child's birthday party. I'm not saying watching a movie or getting online can't be part of a restful activity, but we need to put some thought and intentionality to the question: What activities truly leave me feeling relaxed afterwards?

A Practical Approach: Activities for Relaxing

Here are some ideas to try:

- taking a nap
- playing a family game
- going for a walk (alone or alongside someone)
- reading a book (not related to work)

- watching a movie or television show
- reading a magazine, newspaper, or article online
- writing letters or thank-you notes
- baking cookies
- gardening
- sitting and talking with someone
- calling a friend or family member

Let this short list of ideas be a springboard for listing your own restful activities. Introverts like me tend to be recharged by alone activities, while extroverts like my husband find time spent with other people restorative. I know baking cookies wouldn't be on my list, but my friend says that's what she likes to do to unwind. My husband and I have found a few comedians we really enjoy watching. Laughter can be great medicine for a weary soul!

Your ideas may look very different, but the important concept is to begin planning for rest. Put it into your schedule and guard it. Your children need to see this priority in your life as a follower of Christ. While we now live in freedom and aren't required to do it on a certain day for specific periods, our God calls us to regularly practice rest.

Once we have established a pattern of rest in our lives, we are ready to begin teaching this habit to our children. Jesus helped his disciples understand the value of Sabbath, and we can learn from his example.

TRAINING

1. Jesus trained his disciples about the value of rest.

When the disciples returned from independent ministry, Jesus suggested they take time to be alone: " 'Let's go off by ourselves to a quiet place and rest

139

awhile.' He said this because there were so many people coming and going that Jesus and his apostles didn't even have time to eat" (Mark 6:31).

We find later in Mark 6 that the crowds followed them, and Jesus and his disciples ended up feeding five thousand people instead of getting away to a quiet place. He taught his disciples to pursue rest but not at the expense of divine opportunities. Even though Jesus and his disciples were weary, he provided food for hungry people, but he also taught that choosing to withdraw to a quiet place was a good thing.

When my kids threw tantrums, got overtired, or experienced a few days with packed schedules, they often needed some time alone. Usually they didn't recognize they needed to withdraw, so my husband and I would lovingly mandate a rest.

At times our children need us to instruct them to have some alone time. Often my kids fell asleep soon after being asked to rest. Upon waking they would realize how much their bodies needed some sleep. It's our responsibility to teach them that while God doesn't sleep, he designed us for rest.

We can share with them some of the truths we learned about Jesus in this chapter. He was never in a hurry, valued people over activities, and remains our true source of rest. In addition we can tell them about times in our lives when we packed too much in our schedules and how it affected us physically, emotionally, and spiritually.

Early in our church-planting days, my husband needed administrative assistance. He asked me to help with paperwork, bulletins, e-mails, and other tasks. I thought it wouldn't be a problem since for the first time in my life, I would have all four kids in school! With that mentality, I piled too much on my plate. I usually say I like to carry a platter rather than a plate because I'm a task-oriented kind of gal who likes to get involved! But when I added "administrative assistant" to my task list, even my platter began to overflow.

Our kids were all transitioning to new schools, and I signed up to volunteer in each of their schools or classes. I still led a Bible study and participated in an international cooking class, and cleaning, cooking, and laundry didn't evaporate from my to-do list. Suddenly I was drowning. I began to resent my husband for asking more of me with church-plant demands. It strained our marriage, stressed me out, and left me with no margin when one of my twins began to have significant health problems. She missed a lot of school, and going to doctors' appointments felt like a full-time job. Trying to keep all those balls in the air, I hit a wall emotionally.

Things got better as we found the problem with my daughter's lungs and got the right medication. I also decreased my volunteer work and asked my husband to hire some clerical help for the church. These small changes paid big dividends toward my spiritual well-being. It also enabled me to love and serve others with less of a Martha attitude! And I have been able to share this story with my children when they want to pile too much on their plates.

Many times life can be much more complicated than this illustration. Balancing work, parenting, and caring for a home can leave us feeling as if no easy solutions exist. One of my dear single-mom friends understands the principle of rest but struggles to live it out in the midst of life's many demands. For others, trying to meet deadlines at work or caring for a sick child or family member reminds us that not every season of our life will show a balance between rest and work. The important thing is to do what we can to find rest and trust that our overbusyness will last only a season.

A Practical Approach: Talking with Your Child About Planning for Rest

As you help your child navigate his own schedule, you can show him how to plan for rest. When signing up your child for activities, include her or him in the dialogue. Discuss:

- How will a recreational league, which involves less commitment and intensity, versus a travel team, which requires more commitment and weekends away, affect time for margin and rest?

- How many events or responsibilities each week might make him feel overwhelmed?
- What effect will music lessons, sports commitments, church activities, and family responsibilities have on his ability to take time to obey God's principle of rest?
- What kind of activities help him feel rested?

Include in your conversation a story of time when you were overextended. Talk about how your lack of margin affected your ability to rest. How did it affect your relationships with God and others?

2. Jesus included his disciples in times of spiritual retreat.

While Jesus modeled rest for his disciples by going off alone at times, he also included them in some of his spiritual retreats. He took only Peter, James, and John to a mountainside where he revealed himself more fully through the transfiguration (Mark 9:2-3). He celebrated holidays like the Passover with them as time to stop and remember what God had done. School breaks, holidays, and family vacations can be great restorative times. While these may not be spiritual retreats, you can make a God a priority during your times of rest by talking about him and doing restful activities that honor him: "So whether you eat or drink, or whatever you do, do it all for the glory of God" (1 Corinthians 10:31). Vacations and holidays can include rest that gives glory to God.

For example, as you're out hiking, talk about God's creation. When you're at an amusement park or doing something else fun, mention how much God loves celebration and fun. During holiday celebrations, read the portions of the Bible that explain why we take time out of our routine to pause and remember.

While Sabbath observance isn't a requirement, taking a day to focus on rest isn't a bad idea. With the frenetic pace of life, helping our children learn to pause is a gift we offer them. I admit our kids weren't too keen when we introduced some restful ideas for our family on a weekly basis. Often our children aren't excited about change, especially if we introduce it after they have established habits without limitations. But over time they have discovered the value of rest and peace.

One day, I noticed the house was really quiet. This wasn't normal in the Spoelstra home. Usually there is roughhousing, laughter, kids in and out the doors, and some sort of disagreement about whose turn it is to unload the dishwasher. I scanned the living room, looking up over my laptop screen. My husband was on his computer, two daughters were glued to their handheld electronic devices, and I rightly guessed the other two kids were downstairs watching television. It made for a peaceful Saturday afternoon but didn't leave me with that happy, satisfied feeling a parent gets when she observes a beautiful moment. You know those times when you see your kids cuddling with each other, they say a sweet prayer to Jesus, or they actually put away the game after they played it without being reminded?

This time I questioned whether our family might be a little too plugged in. While I enjoy technology (especially on long road trips), I want to be sure we don't lose that family connectedness that comes from interacting by doing restorative activities together. My husband and I talked later and came up with a plan to be more intentional about spending time together as a family that required no electrical cords or rechargeable batteries.

A Practical Approach: Unplugging as a Family

Start Simple. We decided that we would begin by declaring one media-free day each week. Sundays seemed like the best fit for us: no TV, movies, video games, electronic handheld devices, or even laptops. Since Sunday is the day we attend a church service, often have people over, and love to take naps, it was the most natural time to cut out media. After calling a family meeting, discussing our reasons, and presenting the plan, the kids moaned and groaned a little but eventually hopped on board.

Be Prepared. I have to admit, the first Sunday felt weird. I am addicted to checking my e-mail. When my kids were getting on one another's nerves, I couldn't suggest they watch a show or play on their phones. But we dusted off the board games, went for walks, and planned simple outings. Through media-free days we rediscovered the joy of activities that take only a little more effort than pressing a power button. You can really engage the hearts of your kids when you are part of the fun. Depending on your children's ages, have a family dance party in the living room, play hide and seek or flashlight tag, throw a ball outside, take a family bike ride, or read a well-written missionary story.

Practice What You Preach. Even when you are tempted, be sure you follow the rules as well. Since my husband is a pastor, his day off is Monday. Sunday night he and I would traditionally stay up late and watch a movie together after the kids went to sleep. We debated making an exception for ourselves. After thinking it over, we realized we could come up with some activities for ourselves that didn't include media. We found just sitting on the couch talking, playing a card game, going for a late-night walk, or reading good books and magazines together was good for us too.

❧❧❧

The sacrifice of planning, resting, and powering down has been well worth it. Our children are learning to set limits for themselves and see the benefits of depriving themselves of something they want for a short time for a greater good. The memories we are creating by interacting together through simple, shared activities has been priceless.

The prophet Jeremiah wrote,

> This is what the LORD says:
> "Stop at the crossroads and look around.
>   Ask for the old, godly way, and walk in it.
> Travel its path, and you will find rest for your souls."
> (Jeremiah 6:16)

While media is a great tool for families to communicate, limiting it by taking a day to "ask for the old, godly way, and walk in it" every week may be one of the best things to do at whatever crossroad you're at in the parenting journey.

I'm not proposing that every family needs to go media-free on a weekly basis. God led us to that decision for our family. He may be leading yours in a different direction to incorporate rest into your family's spiritual rhythm. The mode in which we practice rest isn't as important as our intentional pursuit of God's heart in implementing it.

Depending on their personality types, our children won't usually pursue rest. We need to model for them a pace of life and relaxed attitude toward our schedules. By discovering leisure activities that are restorative to us, we show them firsthand the need for balance. As we guard against the tendency to overwork, they see us valuing relationships and peace of mind over tasks.

Then we must go a step further by teaching them how to incorporate rest into their lives. We can help them learn to make decisions about their schedules, include them on spiritual retreats, and help them see the benefits of taking a day each week to adopt some limits on work for the purpose of rest.

My son quit piano lessons in seventh grade after begging to switch to the drums. He enjoys playing in our worship band but in the last few years has meandered back to the piano quite a bit. He plays by ear and finds it very relaxing. I often hear familiar songs he has learned from his favorite bands coming from the room where our piano is located. At nineteen, Zach has a pretty taxing schedule with college courses, volleyball practice, and campus ministry involvement. He finds that after hours of study or a hard workout, sitting down at the piano is a way to unwind and rejuvenate. When he was young, he hated to practice piano. With time and maturity, he now finds it soothing and restful!

A Practical Approach: Restful Family Activity Experiment

One way to get intentional about helping your child determine his or her language of rest is to experiment. Try out some potentially restful activities either together or individually. Then evaluate to see how each family member rated the activity on a scale of how they felt afterward. Here are some places to start.

Try one or more of these ideas either individually or with all family members participating together. Start with at least thirty minutes per activity.

- Spend time in nature.
- Read. (Read a book out loud or have all members silently read different materials.)
- Play an instrument. (Other family members could listen.)
- Color, paint, or complete an art project.
- Take a walk.
- Another idea: _____

After completing an activity, use the following worksheet to evaluate how restful it was for each family member and decide which ones work best for your family. If certain members are energized by different ideas, rotate them on a regular basis.

Family Activity Evaluation Sheet

After spending thirty minutes in a restorative activity (either individually or with all family members), evaluate how restful the activity on each of the following scales, with 5 being most restful and 1 being least restful.

Participating in this activity took my mind off other responsibilities and concerns:

1   2   3   4   5

After the activity, physically I felt more energized and relaxed:

1   2   3   4   5

I felt calmer emotions during and after the activity:

1   2   3   4   5

I thought about God (even for a few moments) during or after:

1   2   3   4   5

I believe doing this more often would benefit my soul and spirit:

1   2   3   4   5

As we train our children to regularly stop working to rest, we help them find a closer relationship with Jesus. We've seen how he calls us to come to him when we are tired and weary, to take on his "light" burden. I pray my children will not follow the world around them that moves at such a fast speed. Psalm 39:6a reminds us that when we spin our wheels, "we are merely moving shadows, / and all our busy rushing ends in nothing."

Eventually our children will have to make their own decisions about rest. They are not our report cards. We aren't called to be sure they learn to rest as adults. But we are to live as examples to them as Christ-followers and teach them. While he may not get worn out, we do. He designed us to stop our work, reflect, remember him, and rest.

Discussion Topics

Group Discussion Questions

- What activities did you identify that are restorative to your soul?

- In what areas have you set limits on your family schedule to build margin for things that come up?

- If you could teach your child one thing about God's call to rest, what would it be?

- If you implemented some regular patterns of rest as a family, what resistance do you think you would face from other family members?

Getting into God's Word

- Read Psalm 121:1-4 and Isaiah 40:28 on pages 127–28. What do these passages teach us about God's sleeping habits?

- Read Genesis 2:2-3 and Exodus 20:8-11. What might be God's heart behind his example and command to rest?

- What are some specific guidelines God gave about Sabbath rest, according to Isaiah 58:13-14?

- Read Matthew 11:28-30. In what ways does this verse encourage you as a parent?

- Which one of these three principles from Jesus's example most resonates with you and why?

1. Jesus was never in a hurry (Mark 1:9-13; 1:45; 3:13; 6:45-46; 10:13-14).

2. Jesus showed us how rest moves us from activity to relationship (Luke 10:38-42).

3. Jesus taught us God's heart behind the Sabbath (Mark 2:27-28).

(If time allows, read each of the corresponding passages and discuss insights you gain about rest from the verses.)

- Read Hebrews 10:1, 9 and Galatians 3:24. Explain how the new covenant replaces the old according to these passages, and others you may have studied. Discuss any questions you have about how this affects our observance of the Sabbath.

- What is something from God's Word that the Holy Spirit used in this chapter to convict or inspire you to make a change in how you model and/or train your child to regularly practice rest?

Digging Deeper

- Read Hebrews 4:1-13. What are some practical ways we can follow the command of verse 11 to "do our best to enter that rest"?

- Read Isaiah 40:28-31. What attributes of God do you find in these verses? What do you learn about people in this passage? What truths found here relate to your current circumstances?

CHAPTER 7

GIVING BACK TO GOD

One day my daughter Rachel, who was in second grade at the time, came to me with tears in her eyes. She pointed to a picture in a book that guides families in praying for different countries of the world. It showed a child sleeping on the street. I hadn't realized the book contained this page for those children around the world who had no home. Rachel wanted to know if some children really lived like the one in the picture. She began to sob as I explained that many kids around the world did not have the clean water, warm homes, or daily food that we take for granted. Then she asked if we could go and find these children and bring all of them to our house.

After telling her that many of the children live very far away, I reminded her of the two children in Guatemala we sponsor and pray for regularly. This cheered her a bit, but my daughter's cushioned world broke a little that day as she began to comprehend the harsh realities of poverty.

Most children possess a tender compassion for others who live without the basic provisions of food, clothing, and shelter. But our kids often don't know what's really happening across the globe, on the other side of town, or even just down the road. Insulated by their world of abundant food, clothing, and entertainment, they can become consumed with their own wants. While we want to protect the sweet innocence of our children, we also must help them look beyond themselves to see the needs of others.

The Bible tells us that God, who made everything and owns it all, is rich. Psalm 50:10 assures us that God "own[s] the cattle on a thousand hills." When the psalmist wrote this, he was illustrating that God didn't need the animal sacrifices that Israel offered to him. Similarly, God doesn't need any money from us; he simply doesn't want us to miss out on the blessing of generosity. Just as he asked the Israelites to make sacrifices with grateful hearts, he asks us to honor him with our resources out of our thankfulness for all he has provided. Psalm 50:14 instructs, "Make thankfulness your sacrifice to God, / and keep the vows you made to the Most High." And Philippians 4:19 assures us, "This same God who takes care of me will supply all your needs from his glorious riches, which have been given to us in Christ Jesus."

God's wealth can't be measured. He is the source of everything we call our own. In order to help our children see God as our provider, we must first see our own resources as the overflow of his wealth. He is a generous God. We can never outgive him. When we share the bounty that God has given us, we reflect his character to others. Take a moment to reflect:

- How has God been generous in your life?
- What difference have his material and spiritual blessings made in your life?

Although our daughter had a generous heart when thinking about poor children in the world, many other times she and our other children have been upset when we wouldn't buy them something, from a toy to a cookie. When the twins were toddlers, I observed them at Sunday school one day when they didn't know I was watching. Abby played with a toy but then got up and moved on to the coloring table. Another child in the class scooped up the toy after Abby walked away only to be accosted by Sara. "That's my sister's!" she insisted as she grabbed the toy from the child. I couldn't believe this girl who frequently squabbled with her twin got so hostile about reclaiming her sister's discarded plaything. All of our children struggle with sin and have a natural bent to heap up resources for themselves—just as Sean and I do. Just as we all do.

As parents we recognize the need to model and train in the area of generosity. It is not something we come by naturally. Our human tendency to be possessive is apparent from a very young age. While God created us in his image, sin affected everything: "Against its will, all creation was subjected to God's curse. But with eager hope, the creation looks forward to the day when it will join God's children in glorious freedom from death and decay" (Romans 8:20-21). This passage goes on to describe creation as groaning with an intensity like that of labor pains. When my children are selfish and won't share, I admit I want to scream like a woman needing an epidural! I wait with eager hope for the day when we are all free from valuing stuff over people.

Rather than give ourselves a bad parenting grade, as I wanted to do that day when I observed my girls in Sunday school, we must focus our energy on modeling and training in generosity. Their attitude and practice related to money affect not only their spiritual lives but also their material decisions and future independence.

MODELING

Let's look again at the life of Jesus to see what he taught us about generosity. If we want our children to become givers, we must provide an example for them to follow that includes regular habits of contribution.

1. Jesus taught that giving requires sacrifice.

Jesus called his disciples' attention to the sacrificial giving of a poor widow:

> Jesus sat down opposite the place where the offerings were put and watched the crowd putting their money into the temple treasury. Many rich people threw in

large amounts. But a poor widow came and put in two very small copper coins, worth only a few cents. Calling his disciples to him, Jesus said, "Truly I tell you, this poor widow has put more into the treasury than all the others. They all gave out of their wealth; but she, out of her poverty, put in everything—all she had to live on." (Mark 12:41-44 NIV)

Notice the contrast between the rich people and the poor widow. The rich gave large amounts out of their wealth, but the poor widow gave two very small copper coins—*everything* she had.

Jesus knows our tendency to give our leftovers, even if those scraps seem like a lot of money compared to others'. I'm guilty too. When Sean and I first got married, we lived in Canada where I had to wait months for the immigration paperwork to be processed before I could legally work. Being fresh out of college, Sean worked as a youth pastor, and we struggled to make ends meet while I could do nothing to help fiscally. After the flurry of my days in college, making pies and keeping a tiny apartment clean left me fretting over our small expenses.

One week I added everything up and declared that we would have to choose between tithing on Sunday and paying rent on Monday. Sean, who has the gift of faith, assured me God would provide, but I, who am inclined to crunch numbers and make a persuasive argument, told him I preferred not to become homeless. I laugh now at my dramatics over what seems like such an inconsequential amount of money against the backdrop of two decades of expenses such as diapers, braces, and car repairs. Ultimately, using all my reason and logic I convinced Sean not to give that Sunday.

That evening before our rent was due, he pulled out an envelope a widow at church had given him that morning. It had slipped his mind in the frenzy of the day. He opened it to find five one-hundred-dollar bills and a note from her mentioning that the Holy Spirit had prompted her to pay our rent that month.

I was astounded. I believed in giving—at least as long as I could pay all my other bills. The memory of this incident has stayed with me through twenty years of financial ups and downs. When we sacrifice like the widow with the two copper coins by participating in Spirit-led giving to the church, missions, or individuals, we get to glimpse God's supernatural and provisional hand in our lives. Giving is much easier when it comes out of excess, as was the case with the rich people who threw large amounts in the offering. Jesus, however, calls us to give sacrificially. While Scripture tells us to plan and exercise good judgment (Luke 14:28), may we not forget that Jesus applauded cheerful giving (2 Corinthians 9:7).

Jesus also modeled sacrificial giving for us. In 2 Corinthians we read, "You know the generous grace of our Lord Jesus Christ. Though he was rich, yet for your sakes he became poor, so that by his poverty he could make you rich" (8:9). Jesus took on spiritual poverty to make us rich in our relationship with God. He left his Father, put on humanity, and came to earth to pay the price for our sin.

On that day early in our marriage when I made the logical decision to withhold our money in order to pay the rent, I missed the opportunity to honor God first. Proverbs 3:9-10 tells us,

> Honor the LORD with your wealth
> and with the best part of everything you produce.
> Then he will fill your barns with grain,
> and your vats will overflow with good wine.

As we offer God the first portion of our resources, he promises to take care of us.

Since that day when God provided our rent, I've watched him consistently take care of our family. Yet I must admit that I still struggle with worry about money. We should be mindful that our children watch how we give.

Do we have eyes to see needs around us? When the offering comes around at church, do we put anything in it? I have found that in order to make giving a priority, I must make our tithe the first contribution from each paycheck. Sometimes I do this online through my bank to be sure I don't forget. At one point, my kids began to ask why they never saw us put anything in the offering. I realized I needed to explain how we give so they knew we always contributed.

As we model sacrificial giving, we can teach our children that God calls us to make sacrifices not to spoil our fun but to allow us to see his supernatural provision.

- When have you made sacrifices in order to give generously?
- How did that experience enrich your spiritual life?

2. Jesus doesn't want us to worry about money but to trust God to provide for our needs.

Not only does Jesus call us to be sacrificial but he also asks us not to worry about material needs:

> Therefore I tell you, do not worry about your life, what you will eat or drink; or about your body, what you will wear. Is not life more than food, and the body more than clothes? Look at the birds of the air; they do not sow or reap or store away in barns, and yet your heavenly Father feeds them. Are you not much more valuable than they? Can any one of you by worrying add a single hour to your life?
>
> And why do you worry about clothes? See how the flowers of the field grow. They do not labor or spin. Yet I tell you that not even Solomon in all his splendor was dressed like one of these. If that is how God clothes the grass of the field, which is here today and tomorrow is thrown into the fire, will he not much more clothe you—you of little faith? So do not worry, saying, "What shall we eat?" or "What shall we drink?" or "What shall we wear?" For the pagans run after all these things, and your heavenly Father knows that you need them. But

seek first his kingdom and his righteousness, and all
these things will be given to you as well. Therefore do
not worry about tomorrow, for tomorrow will worry
about itself. Each day has enough trouble of its own.
(Matthew 6:25-34 NIV)

Notice that this passage speaks about the material needs we often worry
about, including food, drink, and clothing. I once heard someone say, "Worry
is like a rocking chair. It gives you something to do, but it doesn't really get you
anywhere." Over the course of raising four children, I've worn some grooves in
the floor with my worry rocking chair. I desire to obey the command of Christ
to believe God when he says that worry can't add a day to our lives and that
unbelievers chase after material things. Even though God has always provided
in my life, new tests come regularly that push my worry buttons.

The kids keep growing and needing more food and bigger clothes.
Water pipes burst under houses. Dishwashers break. Washing machines leak.
Unbudgeted expenses, such as college applications and standardized test fees,
come up. All of these things happened around the Spoelstra house this year!
You could make your own list of things that push your worry buttons. How
effective have you found your worry rocking chair to be in tackling those
challenges?

Our true beliefs are revealed where our theology meets our reality. Will
we walk by sight, choosing to worry and scheme about our finances? Or will
we walk in faith that God will provide as we continue to put him first—even
when unexpected financial crises knock on our doors?

Children can sense our tension levels. All too easily they can emulate our
money anxiety as they get older. One day, when my son came home and fell
onto the couch, his expression made me think something was very wrong.
I asked him if he had problems at school, work, or his sports team. He said
he'd bought prom tickets that day, and his bank account was low. At church
he had been attending a class for teens on finances, including budgeting and
planning. Those tickets threw off all the neat little categories he had made, and

his engineering brain loves neat categories. He said he was concerned about how to pay for his tuxedo rental with the prom coming up in just a few weeks. He knew he didn't have enough.

I told him that we would be happy to pay for his prom attire. I wondered why he hadn't asked his dad and me for help. As parents, we didn't want him stressed out with money issues while he was still in high school. He had the rest of his life to balance a budget and face the fiscal responsibilities of adulthood. For now, we want to come alongside him and be a resource to help him.

I also asked him if he had prayed about these needs. He confessed that he had spent more time trying to figure out the problem than praying or asking for help. The apple doesn't fall far from the tree! We had a quick but sweet moment of prayer together.

This boy who looks like his daddy inherited his momma's tendency to stress over money. I, too, can get busy trying to strategize how to meet money demands myself rather than ask my Father for help. This encounter reminded me that Jesus doesn't want me to worry, because he has promised to take care of me, and his Father owns the cattle on a thousand hills!

- Can you think of a time when a need seemed overwhelming, but God provided in a supernatural way?
- What joy have you experienced when God prompted you to give to another and you realized how the Lord used you to answer a prayer in that person's life?

Jesus taught us to give sacrificially and to stay worry-free about needs, but what exactly are we required to give? Are we under Old Testament tithing laws? What pattern of giving does God want for my family?

3. Jesus encouraged us to make eternal investments regularly and in proportion to income.

In the Old Testament law, Israelites gave 10 percent of their income to the temple. Sometimes it was money; other times it included goods: "One-tenth of the produce of the land, whether grain from the fields or fruit from the trees, belongs to the LORD and must be set apart to him as holy" (Leviticus 27:30).

These tithes were collected to support the Levites and priests who performed the offerings and served as spiritual overseers in the community. An additional tithe was collected to help the poor as well as the Levites: "Every third year you must offer a special tithe of your crops. In this year of the special tithe you must give your tithes to the Levites, foreigners, orphans, and widows, so that they will have enough to eat in your towns" (Deuteronomy 26:12).

God's law for generosity did not begin and end with the tithe in the Old Testament law. He also encouraged people to be aware of the needs of others and to give generously to them: "If there are any poor Israelites in your towns when you arrive in the land the LORD your God is giving you, do not be hardhearted or tightfisted toward them. Instead, be generous and lend them whatever they need" (Deuteronomy 15:7-8).

While the old covenant has been replaced with a new way of living through Christ, Old Testament principles give us insight into God's heart for giving:

- Giving should be the best of what we have (Proverbs 3:9-10).
- Giving should be based on our income. It is a percentage rather than an arbitrary fixed amount (Leviticus 27:30).
- Giving should be a regular habit just as we regularly earn wages (Leviticus 27:30).
- Giving should sometimes include special offerings or be in response to particular needs not included in our regular giving pattern (Deuteronomy 15:7-8; 26:12-13).

We are no longer bound by a 10 percent rule. But these guidelines provide a framework for how God intends for us to exercise generosity. Jesus never lowered Old Testament standards; he always raised the bar: "You have heard that our ancestors were told, 'You must not murder. If you commit murder, you are subject to judgment.' But I say, if you are even angry with someone, you are subject to judgment!" (Matthew 5:21-22a). Similarly, he equated lust with adultery. Jesus affirmed, "Don't misunderstand why I have come. I did not come to abolish the law of Moses or the writings of the prophets. No, I came to accomplish their purpose" (Matthew 5:17).

Jesus again ups the ante when it comes to giving: "Don't store up treasures here on earth, where moths eat them and rust destroys them, and where thieves break in and steal. Store your treasures in heaven, where moths and rust cannot destroy, and thieves do not break in and steal. Wherever your treasure is, there the desires of your heart will also be" (Matthew 6:19-21).

Jesus didn't say, "Follow your heart and put your treasure where you feel like it." Our hearts are prone to wander. God's Word tells us they can deceive us (Jeremiah 17:9). Instead the Lord calls us to intentionally put our money into what we want our hearts to pursue.

If I desire to care about others trapped in a cycle of poverty, I should make eternal investments in organizations helping the poor. In the same way we follow a stock we have invested in, we will begin to perk up and listen when we hear about the country or organization where we have given resources. Our church partners with a children's center in Guatemala, and our family sponsors children there. When Guatemala is in the news, I listen a little more intently because it affects a place we feel a part of.

- What eternal investments have you made with your money?
- How has your heart begun to track the church, organization, country, or individual where you have given?
- If you asked your children how your family honors God with money, what would they say?

4. Jesus taught about some of the dangers associated with money.

Jesus never said money was bad. Many great men and women of faith were wealthy. Abraham, Job, and King David lived with abundance. People often misquote the Scriptures about money being evil. It doesn't say that! First Timothy 6:10 does say, "The love of money is the root of all kinds of evil. And some people, craving money, have wandered from the true faith and pierced themselves with many sorrows." Notice the key words in this verse: "*The love of money* is the root of all kinds of evil." Jesus warns that when money captures our hearts more than God does, we are headed for trouble. He knows it won't satisfy.

I think about times when I got a new outfit, went on a trip, or enjoyed the computer that money provided. The pleasure might have been wonderful, but it was fleeting. Jesus told a story to illustrate the dangers of loving money:

> A rich man had a fertile farm that produced fine crops. He said to himself, "What should I do? I don't have room for all my crops." Then he said, "I know! I'll tear down my barns and build bigger ones. Then I'll have room enough to store all my wheat and other goods. And I'll sit back and say to myself, 'My friend, you have enough stored away for years to come. Now take it easy! Eat, drink, and be merry!'"
>
> But God said to him, "You fool! You will die this very night. Then who will get everything you worked for?"
>
> Yes, a person is a fool to store up earthly wealth but not have a rich relationship with God. (Luke 12:16-21)

Jesus wants us to understand that joy comes with generosity rather than with bigger barns. We are accountable for the resources God entrusts to us. Jesus warns us not to neglect a rich relationship with God in our quest for earthly wealth: "No one can serve two masters. For you will hate one and love the other; you will be devoted to one and despise the other. You cannot serve God and be enslaved to money" (Matthew 6:24). If we hope our children won't fall into money traps, we must first take a look in the mirror and ask God to reveal any ugly truth about money's hold on our hearts.

Take a few moments to ask God to reveal if a love of money has crept into your life.

- In what ways does the bigger barns story convict you about your personal pursuit of "more"?
- How have you seen a love of money affect those around you?

5. Jesus taught that motives matter when it comes to giving.

Jesus wanted his disciples to understand that God cares about the heart behind the gifts.

> Watch out! Don't do your good deeds publicly, to be admired by others, for you will lose the reward from your Father in heaven. When you give to someone in need, don't do as the hypocrites do—blowing trumpets in the synagogues and streets to call attention to their acts of charity! I tell you the truth, they have received all the reward they will ever get. But when you give to someone in need, don't let your left hand know what your right hand is doing. Give your gifts in private, and your Father, who sees everything, will reward you. (Matthew 6:1-4)

We often desire that others notice our good deeds. Just as our kids always want us to watch and applaud when they learn a new skill, we also want affirmation for accomplishments. Jesus says *he* will reward us. When we realize we long for others to know and praise us for our contributions, it should cause us to do a heart check. Why are we giving?

Reasons for giving should not include the following:

- tradition
- guilt
- approval of people
- pressure from others
- manipulation of leaders or organizations
- tax benefits alone

God says when our motive is the applause of men, we have our reward in full. So what should be our motivation for generosity? "You must each decide in your heart how much to give. And don't give reluctantly or in response to pressure. 'For God loves a person who gives cheerfully.' And God will generously provide all you need. Then you will always have everything you need and plenty left over to share with others" (2 Corinthians 9:7-8). Motives matter.

This isn't easy. Although the guideline of 10 percent seems small when it's one of ten dollars, the tithe check can seem greatly sacrificial on a larger scale. I know for us it is second only to our mortgage. If we didn't give immediately upon receipt of our paycheck, I know I would be tempted to fall back into my old ways of finding good reasons why we need the money more than we need to obey the Lord. We may think it impossible on our budget to truly follow God with regular giving that is proportionate to our income. But God asks us to test him: " 'Bring all the tithes into the storehouse so there will be enough food in my Temple. If you do,' says the LORD of Heaven's Armies, 'I will open the windows of heaven for you. I will pour out a blessing so great you won't have enough room to take it in! Try it! Put me to the test!' " (Malachi 3:10).

My pastor-husband has challenged many families to put God to the test by offering him the first portion of their income. God doesn't need our money, but he does know that our hearts follow our treasure. If we want to know and love him more, we can start by putting our money toward what we say we value.

- Who is the most generous person you've ever known? What images do you see when you picture this person in your mind?
- What is a practical way you can emulate his or her generosity today?

Before we can give sacrificially to store up treasure in heaven, we first must know where the money goes each month. It's easy just to make money decisions as we go—until we have still more bills at the end of our paycheck. In order to give back to God a portion of our income, we need to know where it's all going.

When someone mentions a budget, I used to envision a complicated spreadsheet. But a budget just means you get more intentional about where you want your money to go. You assign each dollar a category so that instead of feeling guilty for your drive through Starbucks, you know it's allowed because you accounted for it in the budget. A budget can be as complicated or as simple as you like. By knowing where your money goes and deciding to honor God with the first part of your wealth, you'll find God opening his storehouses of blessing.

I never stick with complicated systems, so I've learned to use simple methods. Here is one idea.

A Practical Approach: Tracking Your Spending

Even if you already have a budget, I challenge you to make an envelope for each category and write what you think you spend monthly in this area on the front of it. Then track your spending for one month and put all the receipts for actual expenditures in the envelopes (or write expenditures in a small notebook).

The first time I did this, I was shocked by the amount of money we spent at a drive-thru coffee or fast-food place. It made me aware so I could make changes. You might be surprised to find some major discrepancies between what you think you spend and where the dollars really go.

After tracking your spending for a month, you may be more motivated to create a monthly budget! If so, use the worksheet on the following page. There are also many wonderful software programs and apps that can help you to plan and track your expenses. Mint, EveryDollar, PocketGuard, and YouNeedaBudget (YNAB) are some great programs that can be used online or with applications for smartphones or tablets.

Monthly Budget Worksheet

Home (mortgage, repairs, maintenance, utilities) _____

Daily Living (groceries, toiletries, cleaners) _____

Clothing (shoes, clothes, uniforms) _____

Transportation (payment, repairs, oil changes, gas) _____

Entertainment (movies, dining out, coffee) _____

Kids (clubs, teams, fees) _____

Health (medical, dental, gym memberships) _____

Miscellaneous (haircuts, gifts, mad money) _____

Giving (tithe, sponsoring kids, missionaries) _____

Savings (college, retirement, reserves, saving for car) _____

Debt repayment (credit cards, student loans) _____

Total each month _____

Income each month _____

TRAINING

While I cannot overemphasize modeling generosity, we also must help our children learn to give through intentional instruction. Jesus trained his disciples by assuring them that their sacrifices on earth would be rewarded in heaven. Jesus had an encounter with a rich young religious leader in front of his disciples that is recorded in three of the four Gospels. In Matthew, Mark, and Luke we find the account of a man who asks Jesus what he must do to inherit eternal life. First Jesus mentions the commandments, and the man happily replies that he has followed them all since he was young:

> When Jesus heard his answer, he said, "There is still one thing you haven't done. Sell all your possessions and give the money to the poor, and you will have treasure in heaven. Then come, follow me." But when the man heard this he became very sad, for he was very rich. When Jesus saw this, he said, "How hard it is for the rich to enter the Kingdom of God! In fact, it is easier for a camel to go through the eye of a needle than for a rich person to enter the Kingdom of God!" Those who heard this said, "Then who in the world can be saved?" He replied, "What is impossible for people is possible with God." (Luke 18:22-27)

Jesus isn't saying that the Christ-follower should avoid wealth. Instead he is casting a vision for the greater riches of serving God. As we begin to teach our children in our effort to make disciples at home, we must be careful as we train them in handling money. We don't want them to see money as evil or as our sole aim in life. Instead we want them to view their dollars as a tool that can be used for God's kingdom.

At times we may feel as though the task of teaching our kids to be generous is as impossible as a camel going through the eye of a needle! But God says that with him, nothing is too difficult. We will need a plan, perseverance, and flexibility to train our children to honor God first with their resources. Jesus reminds us that it will all be worth it: "Peter said, 'We've left our homes to follow you.' 'Yes,' Jesus replied, 'and I assure you that everyone who has given up house or wife or brothers or parents or children, for the sake of the Kingdom of God, will be repaid many times over in this life, and will have eternal life in the world to come'" (Luke 18:28-30).

As we teach our children about generosity, may we never lose sight of the fact that everything we have here on earth is temporary. When we invest our money in things that will impact eternity—such as giving to our churches; providing food, shelter, and education for children in need both locally and internationally; supporting local and foreign missionaries who have committed their lives to sharing the gospel; or helping someone who needs assistance or support—Jesus says we inherit eternal life and repayment many times over for any earthly losses. So let's move on to some practical ways we can cast a vision of generosity to the disciples under our roofs.

1. Kids need a regular source of income in order to learn generosity.

It's hard for children to learn to handle money if they don't have any. From the time each of our children turned four, we began an allowance system so they could regularly earn money and learn how to save, spend, and give. Others have argued that children shouldn't be paid to do things around the house since it is everyone's responsibility to help out. While I understand that logic, I don't know anyone else who wants to hire my elementary school child! And without a consistent income, they can't learn to manage money.

We've tried many different systems of chores with corresponding allowances. Our kids' rates of pay increased as they grew older and took on more responsibilities. We phased out allowances at around age fifteen, when they began to get regular paychecks by working at jobs outside our home.

Their first allowances were small. They received three quarters at the end of the week if they had completed a few simple routines that included making their beds, putting away toys, and brushing teeth. At first we used three jars, and later three piggy banks, labeled Save, Give, and Spend. One quarter went into each category at the end of the week. The kids had no idea they were giving God 33 percent! They started out as big givers without even realizing it.

As preschoolers, they enjoyed using their spending quarter to get bubble gum or candy in machines at the grocery store. These had been off-limits until they started earning the quarters, and I remember their big smiles as they experienced the first freedoms that came with earning and spending their own money. As they got older, the three quarters quickly turned into three dollars, and then eventually six dollars each week by their early teens.

Here is the system that worked best for us related to chores.

A Practical Approach: A Chore Board System

We had a "chore board" for each child that we attached to the wall. All four boards hung in a row in the kitchen so that the kids could easily see their responsibilities for the morning and evening, which were written on tags that hung on hooks. In the bottom corner of the board was a box where they put each tag as they completed that task. I could easily see which tags remained on the hooks and which had been completed and were in the box. Many of the tags had simple tasks written on them, such as "brush teeth," "make bed," or "eat breakfast." In addition to these personal tasks, there were four chores that we rotated weekly, giving each child a more significant chore for the week. These included:

- unloading the dishwasher
- spraying and tidying the hall bathroom
- bringing all the laundry from each hamper to the laundry room
- emptying the trash from the car and taking out anything left in it

It was nice to start the day with some of their chores out of the way—and to know that the chore board would help ensure the other tasks were completed by the day's end. I enjoyed being able to ask, "Are your tags done?" instead of "Have you made your bed, brushed your teeth, and unloaded the dishwasher?" And the kids enjoyed the sense of responsibility, independence, and accomplishment that it gave them.

Though the particular chore board we used with our children is no longer being manufactured, you could easily create a board of your own or choose from the many other chore boards and charts that are available online and in stores. The idea is to find a system that works for your family.

Try as many different ways to organize and manage chores as you can until something sticks. (I've pinned a number of other ideas on my Pinterest page: www.pinterest.com/spoelstras/) We often give up too soon. We may be just one attempt away from getting into a good rhythm with helping our children find a sense of accomplishment in earning an allowance. Use the six discipleship steps we've already learned:

1. Spending Time in Prayer. Ask God to give you a creative idea for organizing and managing chores. (Or ask his guidance as you scroll through Pinterest ideas to find the one that will work for you!)

2. Reading God's Word. As you read your Bible, ask God to encourage you in persisting.

3. Growing Through Mentoring. Talk to your mentor about ideas he or she used with his or her kids.

4. Finding Community in the Church. When you get together with people from your church, brainstorm ideas with them.

5. Serving Others. If you serve as part of a larger organization like the

church or a nonprofit group, pay attention to its methods of managing tasks to find ideas to implement on a smaller scale.

6. Taking Time to Rest. In your times of rest and reflection, allow God to encourage you.

A potential pitfall in your plan of chores with compensation might be consistently paying your child. Other parents have told me they always forgot payday or didn't have the right amount of cash or change. My kids always knew when it was Friday and exactly how much I owed. They wanted their money! Sometimes I could put them off for a day or two, but soon one or more of them would hound me to pay them. It's natural: I know that if my paycheck didn't come, I sure would be making a call! Once your children get into the rhythm of working for pay, they will remind you about their money to save, spend, and give.

A Practical Approach: Age-Appropriate Chores

When assigning your children chores, it's important to find age-appropriate work so they don't become frustrated with tasks that don't fit their abilities. Here are some ideas that can help you to create a chart, colored-tag system, or poster:

Chores for children age 4 and older:

- help feed animals
- load or unload spoons from dishwasher
- wipe table
- brush teeth; dress and undress
- pull up blankets on bed
- dust furniture
- fold washcloths or dishtowels
- bring items upstairs or downstairs
- tidy books
- set table (provide a diagram)

- wipe baseboards
- dig and pull weeds (make sure you specifically identify weeds versus plants)
- pick up trash or sticks in yard

Additional chores for children ages 6 to 9:

- fold and put away laundry
- gather dirty laundry and take downstairs
- spray and wipe mirror, sink, and counters in bathroom
- unload dishwasher
- take all items out of car; empty car trash
- basic food prep (grate cheese, snap beans, wash fruit or vegetables)
- put away groceries
- bring in mail to proper place
- empty all small trash cans in home into larger bag
- take out trash
- bring recycling to bin
- feed pet independently
- water plants

Additional chores for children age 10 and up:

- cut vegetables
- load dishwasher
- simple cooking or baking
- vacuum
- rake leaves
- use washer and dryer
- clean out drawers, cupboards, closets
- help clean out refrigerator
- clean showers and toilets
- strip and change beds

While I know kids shouldn't complete chores just for the money, cash is a great incentive. Most of us don't work consistently for free. Compensation motivates us. It also provides a great tool for us as parents to withhold money when work isn't completed. Scripture says that people who don't work don't eat (2 Thessalonians 3:10). Though we could do these tasks ourselves with much less hassle, the extra time and energy we spend to assign chores and then train, oversee, and pay our children will be worth it to help them learn about generosity.

2. Kids need training in spending, saving, and giving in order to handle money wisely.

Once our children get a regular allowance, whether it's three quarters or three dollars a week, we want to help them learn to spend, save, and give wisely.

Spending money. In our fiscal training, we coach them as they spend their money. When Zach was little he wanted to go to the dollar store as soon as he got paid and buy things. Then later he would see Lego sets or higher-priced items he really wanted. I would point out to him that he had spent his money at the dollar store. He began to notice that his cheap items didn't last. He began saving larger amounts before asking to go spend his money.

When his sisters began earning their allowances, they also desired to spend it right away. Zach tried to warn them to save up for something better. He pointed out the benefits of buying things that would last longer and bring greater benefits. When they didn't listen, and I allowed them to buy the dollar-store items, Zach became indignant. "Why are you letting them do it?" he asked me. I told him he had learned through experience, and his sisters would need to gain the wisdom of delayed gratification on their own. While we did not mandate how they used their spending money, we tried to teach them about benefits and consequences of choices.

Saving money. When it came to saving, we wanted them to think of the future. We would remind them of upcoming vacations and encourage them to save for souvenirs. As they got older, they began to save for electronics and eventually cars. The habits they learned as preschoolers set the foundation for money decisions down the road. I pray as they enter college and adulthood, they will continue to spend wisely and save for larger items.

Giving money. Making generosity a normal pattern of life is another goal of the allowance system. Remember that Jesus said the eternal investments we make in his kingdom will have exponential returns. While in the beginning the kids were giving God 33 percent, we eventually recommended the 10 percent guideline. It's easy math. If they made $20, they gave two dollars at church. We never asked them to take a portion of their birthday or Christmas monetary gifts to give. We also explained that their small tax returns included money they had already tithed on.

Aside from their regular giving from allowances and early jobs, we also wanted to nurture generosity that helped them understand the joy of giving: "You should remember the words of the Lord Jesus: 'It is more blessed to give than to receive'" (Acts 20:35b).

A Practical Approach: A Christmas Tradition

One way we helped our children learn the joy of giving occurred during the holidays. Even as small children, they weren't only on the receiving end of gifts. We would all load into the van and drive to—you guessed it—the dollar store. My husband would wait with three of them in the vehicle while I would take them in one at a time with their savings. They would pick out one item for everyone in the family. I would try to look the other way when they chose the gift intended for me. After everyone had a turn, we would head home for individual wrapping sessions. They took such joy in thinking of how their sibling or parent would enjoy their gift. Even at four years old, they felt pretty important choosing and preparing gifts to go under the tree.

We traditionally open most presents on Christmas morning, but Christmas Eve is reserved for these special sibling gifts. They can't wait for their turn to hand out their presents and watch the delight of the recipient. Through saving and spending, they experienced firsthand that it is truly more blessed to give than receive. The dollar-store tradition we've long outgrown, but the ritual of buying for one another and celebrating these gifts on Christmas Eve lives on. Of course, the gifts have moved up in scale as their incomes have increased. Still, they greatly enjoy shopping and wrapping with one another in mind.

Beyond just giving gifts to people we love, generosity reaches beyond our four walls to those in need. Jesus put it this way:

> Give to anyone who asks; and when things are taken away from you, don't try to get them back. Do to others as you would like them to do to you. If you love only those who love you, why should you get credit for that? Even sinners love those who love them! And if you do good only to those who do good to you, why should you get credit? Even sinners do that much! And if you lend money only to those who can repay you, why should you get credit? Even sinners will lend to other sinners for a full return.
>
> Love your enemies! Do good to them. Lend to them without expecting to be repaid. Then your reward from heaven will be very great, and you will truly be acting as children of the Most High, for he is kind to those who are unthankful and wicked. You must be compassionate, just as your Father is compassionate. (Luke 6:30-36)

As we help our children recognize God's compassion in their lives, it will overflow onto others. We must help our kids see that we don't just give to those who can repay us in some way. Jesus calls us to generously bless even our enemies. In order to live out Christ's instruction to show compassion, our kids must first understand how blessed they are and how great the needs are of others around the world. Whenever our kids make comments about what nice things other people have that we don't, Sean and I remind them that we are rich compared to some families.

If we are going to compare ourselves, let's look globally. I want my children to understand the accountability we have as Christ-followers to steward resources. One way to instill that perspective is to help them remember how people across the planet are living. Many lack clean water, adequate medical care, and basic food. If we teach the next generation about generosity, we could communicate Christ's love to the world by eradicating poverty. That may seem crazy, but check out these statistics I found related to this very topic. Though they were gathered a few years ago, they highlight the dramatic results that could be realized with even modest increases in giving:

- The total annual income of American churchgoers is $5.2 trillion.
- American Christians make up 5 percent of worldwide Christians but control half of the Christian wealth.
- It would take only 1 percent of the annual wealth of American Christians to lift the poorest one billion of the world's population out of extreme poverty.
- Two percent of money given in American churches is directed toward overseas mission efforts.
- Instead of a true tithe of 10 percent, the average giving of the American church member is 2.5 percent of their income. If we gave the remaining 7.5 percent of the tithe as American Christian people, it would total $168 billion. One year of faithful giving and distribution overseas would change the world.
- It would only take $65 billion (less than 40 percent of $168 billion) to:

o eliminate the most extreme poverty on the planet for more than one billion people.
o provide universal primary education for children ($6 billion).
o bring clean water to most of the world's poor ($9 billion).
o provide basic health care and nutrition for everyone in the world ($13 billion).[10]

While these are a lot of numbers, the reality of what small percentages of money can do is staggering. Rather than moaning about these statistics, as I have done when my kids have asked for more stuff, we need to take action. If every believer followed the pattern of giving 10 percent of their income, and every church followed suit sharing 10 percent with those in need, the impact would be astounding. I believe it begins at home. We can train our children in Christ's model of sacrificial giving. As we teach them God's challenge to test him in flexing our generosity muscles, we could truly rock the planet!

A Practical Approach: Reach the Poor This Week

Coupled with training in giving regularly and in proportion to what we earn, our children need to hear the stories of how other kids around the world live. I created a website—www.reachthepoorthisweek.com—where parents can receive a weekly story about the real life of a child. It includes prayer requests, ways to get involved, a picture, and a story. Many of these updates are written by children ages ten through twelve. Reading and discussing these short stories at the dinner table on a weekly basis helps my children to remember that they are wealthy in many ways. It also inspires them to help others.

One of the stories about a child with special needs gave my youngest daughter, Rachel, an idea. She partnered with a friend in setting up a lemonade stand. All the benefits would go toward a special bike that was needed for a child with disabilities in their class at school. They made a sign and raised money to give to this family. Rachel beamed when the mother of the child thanked her.

As you train your child in generosity, remember that he or she can't learn regular and proportionate giving without an income. In coaching our kids, we can also teach them about wise spending, saving, and giving.

- How have you trained your children in generosity?
- Which idea mentioned in this chapter seems like something that you could adapt to work in your family?

Discussion Topics

Group Discussion Questions

- Share about a generous person who affected your life.

- How did your parents teach you to manage money?

- Think of a time when you were able to give anonymously. How did it feel to be able to provide for a need knowing only God saw it?

- If you could teach your child one thing about handling money, what would it be?

- What are you most scared you would have to give up if you truly lived on a budget?

Getting into God's Word

- Read Psalm 50:7-15. What do we learn about God's resources and his expectation of our sacrifices?

- Read Philippians 4:19 on page 152. What does God promise to take care of in our lives? How would you explain the difference between needs and wants to a preschooler, an elementary school child, or a teenager?

- Which one of these five principles from Jesus's example most resonates with you and why?

1. Jesus taught that giving requires sacrifice. (Mark 12:41-44; 2 Corinthians 8:9; Proverbs 3:9-10)

2. Jesus doesn't want us to worry about money but to trust God to provide for our needs. (Matthew 6:25-33)

3. Jesus encouraged us to make eternal investments regularly and in proportion to income. (Leviticus 27:30; Deuteronomy 26:12-13; Deuteronomy 15:7-8; Matthew 6:19-20)

4. Jesus taught about some of the dangers associated with money. (1 Timothy 6:10; Luke 12:16-21; Matthew 6:24)

5. Jesus taught that motives matter when it comes to giving. (Matthew 6:1-4; 2 Corinthians 9:7)

(If time allows, read each of the corresponding passages and discuss insights you gain from the verses about generosity.)

- Read Malachi 3:10. When you have shown generosity, how have you seen God open his storehouses of blessings?

- Read Luke 18:22-30. Do you think Jesus meant that everyone is supposed to give up all earthly wealth to be his follower? Why or why not? What is Jesus trying to communicate through this encounter?

- What is something from God's Word that the Holy Spirit used in this chapter to convict or inspire you to make a change in how you model and/or train your child in the importance of generosity?

Digging Deeper

- Read Matthew 5:17-30. How did Jesus raise the bar on Old Testament law? How do you notice Jesus getting to the heart of matters in these verses? How can you apply this in parenting?

- Read James 1:9-11. What benefits do the rich have? What does this passage say are the benefits of being poor?

- Read Proverbs 30:8-9. How can relate to this prayer for middle ground when it comes to money?

CHAPTER 8
SHARING YOUR FAITH

I hope that my children become Christ-followers who pray, study the Bible, find a mentor, plug into church community, serve, rest, and give. But I also want them to learn to share their story of faith with others. God wants to use us as well as our children to tell others about him so that they can experience his unconditional love, unlimited forgiveness, never-failing hope, and saving grace—both now and for all eternity. As I've said previously, he could use rocks or donkeys or anything to speak out, but Jesus entrusted his message to *us*!

In order to teach our children to share their faith, we need to begin with clarity about our own faith journeys. I'm not talking about being a professional speaker but being able to explain the basic gospel message and what God has done for us: "If someone asks about your hope as a believer, always be ready to explain it" (1 Peter 3:15b). This verse can be intimidating when we think about being ready to "explain" our faith. It can be easier to describe our favorite pizza or our hometown team's season than how God has worked in our hearts and lives!

Sometimes we shy away from talking about spiritual things because

- We don't know how to explain the gospel.
- We are worried we don't have all the answers. (We don't!)

- We know we aren't perfect and don't feel qualified.
- We are nervous about what others will think.

Do any of these reasons strike a chord with you? What are some other things that keep you from sharing your faith and the gospel message with others?

Let's debunk some evangelism myths together and look at Jesus's example and call for us to share our faith with others.

MODELING

I haven't met many Christians who became believers because of fear, force, or threats. Neither have I met many who say that they were argued into the kingdom. Although some use these evangelism tactics, they are rarely effective or winsome. And that certainly wasn't the way Jesus went about it. How did Jesus share God's message, and what was his focus?

1. Jesus established relationships and reached out in love.

As we observe the ministry of Jesus throughout the Gospels, we find him surrounded by people from all different backgrounds. His disciples included women, such as Mary the sister of Lazarus and Martha, who broke tradition by sitting at Jesus's feet. He offered his message of love to religious people such as Nicodemus and tax collectors such as Zacchaeus.

Jesus came to seek and save those who were lost. He ate and established relationships with people from all levels of society, and in the process he shared love and truth. If we want to share our faith with others, we must begin with building true friendship, then loving as Christ did.

I taught English in Japan one summer in college, took Japanese language in college, and adore Japanese culture. I can't help but want to befriend a Japanese woman when I see her at the gym or the grocery store. I usually try to invite her to an international cooking class I'm involved in during which women from all different nationalities get together to cook.

I've had many Japanese friends over the years, and most have now moved back to Japan. One gal in particular became a close friend. I tutored Hidemi in English after I met her at our neighborhood block party when she first moved here. She was actually the one who invited me to the cooking class I've been a part of for over a decade. Over the course of three years she asked me questions about my faith. I shared honest answers with her about my relationship with Christ. One day she told me that she had begun attending a Japanese Christian church so she could understand words spoken in her first language.

I was thrilled when she invited me to come and hear her share her story of faith of Christ and watch her baptism. The tears streamed as she told of her journey and our faith conversations. Throughout our friendship I didn't realize what an impact God was making in her life. Before her family moved back to Japan, all three of Hidemi's children also expressed the desire to become believers, and my husband got the opportunity to baptize her daughter.

I don't know why I was surprised that Jesus worked in such a powerful way in her life through love and friendship. It is his way. Jesus didn't offer canned speeches or overcomplicate the gospel. He pursued real relationships and loved people. He came to save the world, not to judge it (John 3:17).

As disciples we can follow Christ in developing real friendships with no strings and look for opportunities to share. I've had several other friends from Japan who weren't interested in Christ. They weren't projects; they were real friends. We shared experiences and talked about beliefs, but only one decided to follow Jesus.

To share God's message of love like Christ, we must start with living out Romans 12:9a: "Don't just pretend to love others. Really love them." As we befriend others and live out our faith, God will do the incredible work of seeking and saving those who are lost.

2. Jesus said he is "the way" to God.

Jesus spoke boldly to his disciple Thomas: "I am the way, the truth, and the life. No one can come to the Father except through me" (John 14:6).

Living in our culture of tolerance, we may find this concept offensive to others. Christians are often described as narrow-minded if they say that Jesus is the only means by which people can be reconciled to God. These are not our words, but those of Jesus himself. To embrace the gospel is to admit that God's Word trumps even what makes sense to us.

My children have been called "haters" for admitting they believe that Jesus is the only way to God. It is sometimes viewed as unkind to students of other religions to proclaim that Jesus alone restores a right relationship with God. Even several of my children's Christian friends say that other ways to God could be right too. It sounds nice to affirm everyone's beliefs, but it is actually love that compels us to be clear about who Jesus is, why he willingly died on a cross, and what that means for each of us.

When we share the gospel message and what God has done in our lives, we aren't judging others, exerting superiority, or heaping shame on them. We are lovingly letting them know that Jesus is the only way to reconciliation with God and new life. And when we share what difference this has made in our own lives, our words convey sincerity and love—not judgment or self-serving motives.

As we've seen, Jesus didn't go around preaching fire and brimstone; he led with love and relationship. But he also didn't shy away from the truth. Writing about the beginning of Jesus's ministry, Matthew tells us, "From then on Jesus began to preach, 'Repent of your sins and turn to God, for the Kingdom of Heaven is near'" (4:17).

People often use an illustration to suggest that all paths lead to God. They say that we are at the base of a mountain and God is at the top, and we all are taking different paths (religions) to get to the same God. They claim God expresses himself differently to reach everyone. That sounds good, but there are some problems with this illustration. First, as we've seen, Jesus himself said that he is the only way. Second, if God the Father had another method for reconciling us to himself that did not include sacrificing his own Son, it would seem cruel and inconsistent with his nature not to use it. Finally, our

God doesn't ask us to work our way up to him; he came down from heaven in human form to restore the relationship that sin had broken.

One of my Hindu friends invited me over to celebrate a special day in her faith. I was happy to go, eat traditional food, and learn about her religious observances. I didn't argue, invalidate her methods, or criticize her religion in any way. She is my friend. I treated her the way I would want to be treated. But as she talked about her spirituality, she began to ask questions about what I believe. I was able to share about Jesus and his message of love and sacrifice on our behalf.

Real friends respect each other's differences and talk about what they believe as they share life together. I pray my Hindu friend will one day see the truth about Jesus, but in the meantime I share the love of Christ without compromising my beliefs by embracing the idea that all religious roads lead to the same destination.

Jesus is the Lamb of God who takes away our sin and makes it possible for us to live in fellowship with God for all eternity (John 1:29; Revelation 21:27). As opportunities arise for us to share our stories of faith, I pray we will have the courage to communicate this central belief that distinguishes our faith from all others—always speaking with sensitivity, love, and respect.

- What practical ways have you been able to forge relationships with people of other religions?
- How have you witnessed to your faith without being offensive?

3. Jesus shared the gospel message.

Gospel simply means "good news." The good news is that God loves us and made a way for us to be reconciled to him. Because sin separates us from God, he sent his Son to deliver us from the penalty and power of sin and reconcile us to God. When we recognize God's love for us and our sinfulness, then embrace Christ's death on the cross as the sufficient sacrifice for our sin, God forgives us. This gospel is woven throughout the breadth of Scripture.

Here are four points and some Scripture verses that I like to use when explaining the message in simple terms:

1. **God loves us:** "For this is how God loved the world: He gave his one and only Son, so that everyone who believes in him will not perish but have eternal life." (John 3:16)
2. **We all sin and disobey God:** "For everyone has sinned; we all fall short of God's glorious standard." (Romans 3:23)
3. **Christ freed us from the penalty and power of sin and offers us new life:** "He himself is the sacrifice that atones for our sins—and not only our sins but the sins of all the world." (1 John 2:2; see also Romans 5:8 and 2 Corinthians 5:17)
4. **We are invited to accept Christ's offer of forgiveness and new life:** "To all who believed him and accepted him, he gave the right to become children of God." (John 1:12)

My neighbor's daughter heard this message at a backyard Bible club in our garage and decided to believe in Jesus. I knew I needed to have a conversation about her commitment with her mom, who was not a believer. I didn't want her to think we had brainwashed her daughter. So we went out for lunch, and I began to tell her about her daughter's decision to become a Christ-follower. When she inquired what I meant by that term (she had never heard the gospel message before), I explained the simple gospel message that had been presented about God's love, our sin, Christ's payment on the cross, and the need to receive Christ.

Her next statement caught me off guard. She said, "So you are saying I can be a good person my whole life and not go to heaven. But a murderer can believe the truths you just talked about and be forgiven and go to heaven? That doesn't make sense to me."

I was able to share with her that forgiven people, not good people, go to heaven because none of us is good enough for God's holy standard. I admit that it was an awkward conversation. But our friendship continued as we watched each other's children, talked over the backyard fence, and celebrated birthdays together.

Several years later, she told me her marriage was ending and they were moving to another town. I felt impressed by the Holy Spirit to give her a copy of a book by Andy Stanley called *If Nobody's Perfect, How Good Is Good Enough?* It's a small book that concisely explains why the "good people go to heaven" theory lacks biblical support. She called me later to tell me that she had read the book and understood its message; and best of all she had accepted Jesus as her Savior, too.

I had been nervous to give her the book. I didn't want to seem pushy or judgmental, but my heart motive was love. Other times I've felt compelled to invite people to church activities or to be bold when spiritual topics come up in conversation. I've realized that many people truly are searching for hope and truth, and God wants to use us to build relationships with others and share what we know about him and his gospel of grace.

A Practical Approach: Writing Your Faith Story

So what's your faith story? Some people know the hour and the day that they believed the gospel message and put their faith in Christ, and others grew up in the church or simply know they believe but can't pinpoint a specific moment when they started. Either way, our salvation should be more of a present reality than a past experience. It is an ongoing story as God continues the process of making us more and more like Jesus. If we want to help our children learn to communicate their story of faith, we should be ready to give our own answer.

Think through the following questions. Then using these questions as a guide, write out the story of your faith journey. You may want to use a journal, a tablet or computer, or special paper.

- Tell about your childhood view of God. What shaped your early thoughts about who God is?
- Before deciding to follow Jesus, what was your source of truth? In other words, what guided your life decisions? Or if you grew up in the church or don't remember a time when you didn't love Jesus, how did your faith guide your life decisions at a young age?
- What situations or people brought your need for Jesus to the surface or intensified your awareness of this need?
- What were the circumstances of your decision to follow Jesus or fully commit your life to him? Who explained the gospel to you?
- What changes have taken place in your life after receiving Jesus and his gift of grace?
- What has helped you grow in your journey of faith?
- What is God doing now in your life? How are you becoming more like Jesus?
- Do you have a favorite Bible verse that has been especially relevant or meaningful in your life?

After you have identified some of the stories and poignant moments in your own journey of faith, ask God to give you opportunities to share it with others. You also might want to share it with your children (see pages 197–98 for a family activity idea). When sharing your story publicly, you will want to be careful to:

- make the gospel clear
- avoid making negative references to any denomination or religious tradition
- focus on what God has done and is doing rather than spend too much time on past sin stories
- tell what God has done in your life in plain language that anyone can understand, avoiding Christian jargon, such as *born again*, *saved*, or *conversion*

When we aren't sharing a planned testimony at an event or church service, we should wait for moments when the Holy Spirit leads us to tell about our faith experiences authentically. We all know what it feels like when someone is pressuring us for a sale. While it's good to think through the preceding questions and clarify your spiritual journey in your own heart and mind, you certainly aren't working on some kind of a sales pitch.

When we watch movies and television, we don't see the writers and producers on screen stating the tenets of a secular worldview with statements such as "Adultery is fun"; "Material possessions will make you happy"; or "Religion is for the weak-minded." Instead, they draw us in with a story. A well-thought-out, interesting plot captivates us, weaving hints of the ideologies it espouses throughout the storyline. This powerful and effective method shapes the worldview and thinking of millions of people.

As we consider our Christian faith, we passionately want others to know and embrace our Savior and Lord and wonder what will reach our neighbors, family, and friends. We can give them books, invite them to church, and take advantage of opportunities as they arise to talk about our faith and beliefs. Yet we must remember that people are watching the stories of our lives, and those are perhaps the most powerful testimonies of all.

What is the message of your life story? Ask yourself a few questions: How do I respond to and talk about my family members? Do I own up to my mistakes? Do I reflect God's grace when someone treats me unkindly? Does the plot of my life story give evidence of my faith in Christ? How will my attitudes, my words, and my authenticity influence watching people's thinking and worldview? Can they relate? The idea is not to strive for some kind of pie-in-the-sky "my life is perfect because I love Jesus" façade but to authentically follow Jesus and let his presence and power in our lives point others to him.

- What opportunities have you had to share with others your journey of faith?
- Is there a particular person on your heart with whom you are hoping to share your faith journey?

4. Jesus didn't focus on minor points of doctrine.

As we pray and look for opportunities to share our stories, sometimes others will divert the conversation to hypocrisy in the church or whatever issue is currently a hot topic in mainstream media. Other times they may have a tender spot about an area where Christians treated them poorly or judged them. Whenever I've allowed myself to get caught up in minor issues, I've missed the heart of God's gospel of grace in conversation. So how can we stay on track when discussing our faith?

Let's look again to Jesus. He encountered many people who tried to change the subject from his teaching or focus on a minor point. The Pharisees asked him about taxes, and a Samaritan woman he met at a well wanted to discuss the right place to worship:

> "So tell me, why is it that you Jews insist that Jerusalem is the only place of worship, while we Samaritans claim it is here at Mount Gerizim, where our ancestors worshiped?" Jesus replied, "Believe me, dear woman, the time is coming when it will no longer matter whether you worship the Father on this mountain or in Jerusalem. You Samaritans know very little about the one you worship, while we Jews know all about him, for salvation comes through the Jews. But the time is coming—indeed it's here now—when true worshipers will worship the Father in spirit and in truth. The Father is looking for those who will worship him that way. For God is Spirit, so those who worship him must worship in spirit and in truth." The woman said, "I know the Messiah is coming—the one who is called Christ. When he comes, he will explain everything to us." Then Jesus told her, "I AM THE MESSIAH!" (John 4:20-26)

Jesus didn't spend time debating the issue she brought up about the location of worship. Instead he talked about the Father looking for people to worship him in Spirit and in truth and identified himself as the Messiah.

Following Jesus's example, we can use discernment when sharing our faith. When people want to spar over theology or politics, we can ask questions and listen to discern their spiritual temperature. Are they truly seeking answers about life and afterlife, or do they just enjoy argument?

As we read the rest of the Samaritan woman's story, we learn that she believed Jesus and shared her testimony immediately with her entire village (John 4:28-29). This was an indication of her transformation. You see, she had had several husbands and was living with someone she wasn't married to (v. 18); so she likely had come to the well during the heat of the day to avoid the crowd of women who came in the cooler morning or evening times. This woman was not accustomed to interacting with others in the community, but after spending time with Jesus, she boldly shared her faith.

Isn't it freeing to realize that God doesn't call us to save anyone? Our responsibility is only to share the message. It is the Savior, not us, who transforms lives.

- What side issues do people sometimes bring up when discussing Christianity and faith?
- How can you follow Jesus's example of not getting pulled into debates about secondary issues?

TRAINING

Once we have some clarity about our own spiritual journey, we will want to help our children articulate what God has done in their lives. Even before they make a personal decision to follow Jesus or a public profession of faith, we can help them begin to understand the gospel message by finding times within the daily routine to talk about faith in age-appropriate ways:

- **God loves you.** Children of every age need to be reminded that God is crazy about them. Older children and teens can understand that God wants to have a relationship with them.

- **We all make mistakes.** When our children make mistakes or do wrong, we can encourage them by reminding them that everyone sins—including Mom and Dad. When we sin, we can remember that God forgives.
- **Jesus came to bridge the gap between us and God.** At Christmas and Easter we talk about Jesus's coming to earth and giving his life for us, but we can talk about the cross and what Jesus has done for us throughout the year as we go about our daily lives.
- **Receiving Jesus's gift of new life and following him is the way to have a right relationship with God.** When our children initiate this conversation, we should let the Holy Spirit lead. When they express interest, we can be ready to give an age-appropriate answer for the hope we have.

At times our children will initiate spiritual conversations. For my children, the death of a loved one, questions about communion, and watching baptisms have initiated conversations that led to discussions of the gospel. Eventually each child made a personal decision to embrace the truth of the gospel and begin a personal walk with the Lord. One time it was in the car. Another time it was at the kitchen table. Another child prayed to accept Christ's gift of salvation and new life during a bedtime conversation. Then they began to grow in faith through prayer, Bible study, mentoring, church community, serving, resting, and giving. Other children grow in faith through these practices before making an outward profession of faith. Either way, the overflow of our children's love for God often brings a desire to tell others about him—much in the way that they want to tell family and friends when they have good news to share.

Jesus modeled spiritual conversations that met people right where they were in life—without condemnation. He helped people to know God, and he trained his disciples to do the same. We can follow in their footsteps as we train our children to share their faith.

1. Jesus commissioned his followers to make more disciples.

Before leaving his disciples and ascending into heaven, Jesus said, "I have been given all authority in heaven and on earth. Therefore, go and make disciples of all the nations, baptizing them in the name of the Father and the Son and the Holy Spirit. Teach these new disciples to obey all the commands I have given you. And be sure of this: I am with you always, even to the end of the age" (Matthew 28:18-20).

As we saw in an earlier chapter, these final words of Christ are referred to as the Great Commission. We are participating in the Great Commission when we train our children in the faith and, when they are ready, teach them how to "make disciples."

There are many ways children can help others to know and love God, but I'd like to lift up three basic ideas:

> Pray
> Invite
> Share

Pray. It's important to begin with prayer. Thursdays are the days our family prays for people who do not have a relationship with Jesus. As parents we must be sure to set a nonjudgmental tone when praying for those who do not follow Christ. They are not "bad people" or inferior. Rather we want them to experience the love, hope, peace, and joy of having a personal relationship with Jesus—now and for all eternity. Deciding to follow Jesus doesn't mean that all our problems go away and life is easy. It doesn't take long for our children to figure that out. But we can be sure of Christ's final words: "I am with you always" (Matthew 28:20). He will walk with us through every storm and give us purpose and joy in the midst of it.

Invite. As our children attend church, vacation Bible school, or a midweek program or Bible study, they will have opportunities to invite others. As parents, we can come alongside and offer suggestions and plans ahead of time to make this possible. Kids usually think of things at the last minute. By coaching them to think ahead, we can make it easy for their friends to join them in hearing God's Word.

We usually loaded up our van with friends on our way to children's programs, youth group, or other fun faith activities. Encouraging this not only helps your child enjoy church more; it also exposes their friends to the life-changing gospel message. Sometimes seeds are sown that you may never see bear fruit. But I've heard many adults refer to times they visited church with friends as children, sharing the impact it had later in life.

Share. With some encouragement and basic training or instruction, we can help our children think and talk about their faith at every age or developmental stage. Here are some ideas.

A Practical Approach:
Helping Kids Think About and Share Their Faith

Ages 3–7

During these early years of development, children's faith is based on impressions. They are not yet able to give a description of their faith. Their thoughts will be based on stories they have heard and ideas they have picked up from you and others—at home and at church. At this age they are building a foundation for the faith they will have later. Repetition at home and at church can help them grab onto tangible expressions of faith, and connecting these two worlds can help them to see that faith is a way of life.

Having young children draw pictures or engage in simple activities is a great way to help them give expression to their beginning understanding of faith. Provide paper and crayons or markers, then verbally give some age-appropriate prompts such as these:

- Draw a picture of your church.
- Draw a picture of someone who has told you about Jesus.
- Draw a picture of what you think of when you hear about Jesus.
- Draw a picture of something your family does for Jesus.

Ages 8–12

Children aged eight to twelve are beginning to apply logic and reasoning to concrete events, though they still lack the ability to fully understand abstract concepts. For this age group consider these ideas:

- Draw a picture of or write about people who show Jesus's love to others.
- Draw a picture of or write about ways you show Jesus's love to others.
- Draw a picture of or write about ways you worship Jesus.
- When and how have you said yes to Jesus, accepting his gift of love and forgiveness? Draw a picture or write about it.

These prompts can help older children begin to articulate their journey of faith, giving you opportunity to share or review the gospel message with them in simple terms (see page 186) and answer any questions they may have.

Age 12–Teens

From around the age of twelve through the teen years, abstract thinking develops and thoughts become less tied to concrete reality. At this age, a worksheet such as the one that follows can help them think about and write their own faith stories. Using this worksheet at home not only helps our kids articulate their faith stories; it also gives us another opportunity to review the gospel with them and answer questions.

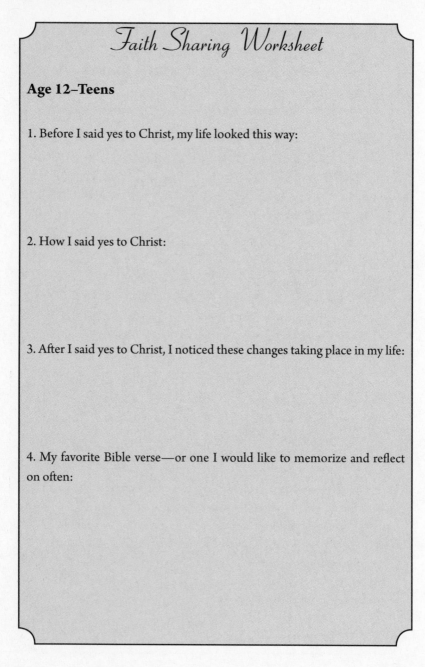

Faith Sharing Worksheet

Age 12–Teens

1. Before I said yes to Christ, my life looked this way:

2. How I said yes to Christ:

3. After I said yes to Christ, I noticed these changes taking place in my life:

4. My favorite Bible verse—or one I would like to memorize and reflect on often:

While a faith story or testimony entails much more than pictures, sentences on a worksheet, or planned activities, we found these things to be helpful tools along the parenting journey. As our children continue to mature, we hope their testimonies will flow out of hearts that love God and want others to experience his love and grace. Preparing a simple description of how following Jesus has changed their lives can help prepare older children for sharing their faith when conversations or other opportunities arise.

The apostle Paul modeled this practice for us when he stood before King Agrippa in Acts 26. He spoke simply, logically, and clearly about his life before salvation, how he met Christ, and what his life was like after his conversion. Paul's testimony takes three or four minutes to read aloud in a conversational manner and can be a good passage to discuss with your child before (or after) talking about your own faith stories.

I encourage you to take some time to share your own testimony with your child as well. As you talk about the transformation that has occurred in your life by following Jesus, your children will learn from your example. Be prepared to listen and also to learn from your child as you talk about faith together!

A Practical Application: Faith-Sharing Family Night

Consider having a family night to talk about and share your faith stories.

Get Ready

- Select the age-appropriate activity or activities you would like to do (pages 194–95). Make one or more copies of the Faith Sharing Worksheet if you have a child or children age twelve or older (page 196).
- Gather some colorful markers and crayons and/or pencils or pens.

- Buy some faith symbols stickers.
- Fill out your own Faith Sharing Worksheet ahead of time (page 196).
- Pray with your spouse. If you are a single parent, invite a prayer partner, friend, or extended family member to be praying for you—or participate with you.
- Set reasonable expectations for varying attention spans.

Get Started

- Start by having a special dessert.
- Open with a short prayer.
- Read aloud 1 Peter 3:15.
- Share your personal testimony.
- Explain the activity or activities.
- Guide your child through the activity. If you have multiple children in different age categories, do one activity at a time. Older children and teens can assist with activities for younger children or participate by offering encouragement.
- End with a family game or movie.

2. Jesus reminded his disciples of the value of the message.

Jesus constantly reminded his disciples that the gospel matters more than anything else in life. Following Christ is not a hobby or a box we check on a survey about our religion. It is worth giving our whole lives to share the gospel with others. Jesus said that all nations need to hear it. That means the Lord might call us or some of our dear children to faraway places to live out this message.

I've had mature Christ-followers tell me they hope their children all live within five miles of them when they grow up. I've also seen parents manipulate situations to try to keep their kids close after college. I admit that sometimes

I want my kids to be happy, healthy, and near me more than I want them to be holy or for God to use them to make disciples. But if we truly believe the gospel is the most valuable truth worth living and dying and for, then we must be willing to go or let go of our children for the sake of this treasure. Jesus described it this way: "The Kingdom of Heaven is like a treasure that a man discovered hidden in a field. In his excitement, he hid it again and sold everything he owned to get enough money to buy the field. Again, the Kingdom of Heaven is like a merchant on the lookout for choice pearls. When he discovered a pearl of great value, he sold everything he owned and bought it!" (Matthew 13:44-46).

Jesus used treasure and an expensive pearl to illustrate that the kingdom of heaven is worth giving up everything else for. When we talk to our kids about faith, we should help them see that God's way is better than any other—especially ours.

My intent is not to heap guilt or shame on you or me. We love our children fiercely, and we should. We just need God's Word to help us remember that the best thing our kids can do is follow Christ. Whether that's on another continent or right down the street from us, our desire should be that they live for God's kingdom instead of building their own.

We can help our children see that making disciples is a calling worth pursuing and one that brings God glory. Telling others about Christ isn't something just for professional Christians and fanatics. In Psalm 107 we read, "Has the LORD redeemed you? Then speak out! Tell others he has redeemed you from your enemies" (v. 2).

I pray my children will be gripped by the calling to share the message of the gospel so that others can discover a rich relationship with God through Jesus. We would be wise to train our children to contemplate the value of the message they have to share. In true love and friendship, we can build a bridge of love between our hearts and those of unbelievers so that Jesus can walk across.

DISCUSSION TOPICS

Group Discussion Questions

- When did you first understand and embrace the gospel message?

- If time allows, have each person in your group share a one- to two-minute testimony of how his or her life has changed since deciding to follow Jesus.

- What gospel-centered conversations have you had with your children?

- What are some reasons you are hesitant to share your faith with others who don't believe in Jesus?

- What ineffective ways of sharing faith have you observed others use that have actually turned people away from Christianity? (Think of social media, judgmental statements, and so on.)

- Is there one person who is far from God whom you are especially burdened to pray for?

Getting into God's Word

- Which one of these six principles from Jesus's example most resonates with you and why?

  1. Jesus established relationships and reached out in love.

2. Jesus said he is "the way" to God. (John 14:6)

3. Jesus shared the gospel message. (John 1:12; John 3:16; Romans 3:23; Romans 5:8)

4. Jesus didn't focus on minor points of doctrine. (John 4:20-26)

5. Jesus commissioned his followers to make more disciples. (Matthew 28:18-20)

6. Jesus reminded his disciples of the value of the message. (Matthew 13:44-46)

(If time allows, read each of the corresponding passages and discuss insights you gain about sharing our faith stories from these verses.)

- Read Psalm 107:2. What are some ways that God has redeemed your life? How have you shared these experiences with others?

- How has the Holy Spirit inspired or convicted you to make a change in how you model and/or train your child in the importance of sharing faith?

Digging Deeper

- Read Acts 26. What are some principles you learn from Paul's testimony before Agrippa?

- What wisdom does Colossians 4:5-6 give us regarding how we are to share our beliefs?

- Read Romans 1:16-17. How does Paul describe his posture toward the gospel? In what ways it is sometimes difficult to stand up for your beliefs in our modern world?

EPILOGUE

As we look over the eight practices to model and train for our children as followers of Christ, it can be overwhelming. Yet Jesus lived out each one as an example for us. He doesn't ask us to accomplish it all today. We have a couple of decades to set an example and instruct our children.

Also, we don't need to measure our effectiveness based on our child's current behavior and choices. Instead we should seek to live and teach:

1. spending time in prayer on a regular basis
2. studying and applying God's Word
3. seeking a mentor to speak into our lives
4. finding community in a local church body
5. serving others sacrificially
6. building times of Sabbath rest into a busy schedule
7. giving back to God a portion of the money we earn
8. sharing our story of faith with others

My prayer is not that you implement every idea in this book. But I do hope that you will be inspired to be intentional and focused on teaching your child what it means to live as a Christ-follower. Adopt at least one or two new practices in your life and begin to cultivate spiritual conversations with your child.

When King David was passing the spiritual baton to his son Solomon, he encouraged him with these words: "And Solomon, my son, learn to know the God of your ancestors intimately. Worship and serve him with your whole heart and a willing mind. For the LORD sees every heart and knows every plan and thought. If you seek him, you will find him" (1 Chronicles 28:9a).

As you train your children in godliness, don't make their behavior your report card. Instead, encourage them to get to know God intimately. Teach them to be seekers of his heart. King David continued, "Be strong and courageous, and do the work. Don't be afraid or discouraged, for the LORD God, my God, is with you. He will not fail you or forsake you" (1 Chronicles 28:20). In parenting, we all make mistakes and feel inadequate at times, especially when it comes to spiritual conversations. We are wise to embrace David's words to his son about being strong and doing the work.

Let's lay aside our excuses and discouragement and begin today by modeling and training. It might mean taking that extra time to read and pray with your child at bedtime even when you're tired. Perhaps the Holy Spirit will nudge you to plan some service projects when you'd rather be out shopping or golfing. It might require getting up a little earlier to pray or reprioritizing your spending in order to practice generosity.

As we obey the Lord's leading to draw our families closer to him, he will be with us. He will not fail or forsake us as we parent the children he has entrusted into our care. As we incorporate new spiritual rhythms in our family's lives, I pray we will experience increased intimacy with him.

NOTES

1. "What Are the Reading Levels of the Bibles on Bible Gateway?" forum post, June 2, 2010, https://support.biblegateway.com/entries/186624 -What-is-the-reading-level-of-the-Bibles-on-Bible-Gateway.

2. *Merriam-Webster's Dictionary*, online edition, s.v. "mentor." www .merriam-webster.com/dictionary/mentor.

3. Dave and Jon Ferguson, *Exponential: How You and Your Friends Can Start a Missional Church Movement* (Grand Rapids: Zondervan, 2010), 58, 63.

4. Ibid., 128.

5. Kara E. Powell and Chap Clark, *Sticky Faith: Everyday Ideas to Build Lasting Faith in Your Kids* (Grand Rapids: Zondervan, 2011), 102.

6. "Who Is Albert Schweitzer," the website of Albert Schweitzer's Leadership for Life, http://aschweitzer.com/abouta.html.

7. Jean M. Twenge and W. Keith Campbell, *The Narcissism Epidemic: Living in the Age of Entitlement* (New York: Free Press, 2009), 16.

8. "Teens Are Feeling More Anxious Than Ever," *Elements Behavioral Health*, accessed March 29, 2016, www.elementsbehavioralhealth.com/ featured/teenagers-are-feeling-more-anxious-than-ever/.

9. Richard Swenson, *Margin: Restoring Emotional, Physical, Financial, and Time Reserves to Overloaded Lives* (Colorado Springs: Navpress, 2004), 13.

10. Richard Stearns, *The Hole in Our Gospel: What Does God Expect of Us? The Answer That Changed My Life and Might Just Change the World* (Nashville: Thomas Nelson, 2009), 216–18.

Dig Deeper into Scripture with Bible Studies by Melissa Spoelstra

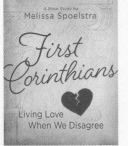

First Corinthians: Living Love When We Disagree
Participant Workbook – ISBN: 9781501801686

Relationships are messy. How can we work out our differences and disagreements with humility and grace, always showing the love of Christ, while still remaining true to what we believe?

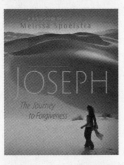

Joseph: The Journey to Forgiveness
Participant Workbook – ISBN: 9781426789106

All of us know what it's like to be hurt or betrayed. God wants us to release our past and present hurts and allow Him to do a supernatural work of forgiveness in our life.

Jeremiah: Daring to Hope in an Unstable World
Participant Workbook – ISBN: 9781426788871

We live in an unstable world where the uncertainties, challenges, and everyday demands of life get us down. Learn to surrender to God's will and rest your hope in Him alone.

DVD, leader guide, and kit also available for each six-week study.

Discover more women's Bible studies at AbingdonWomen.com.

Available wherever books are sold.

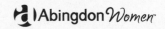